ALCHEMY

GW00673118

POCKET LIBRARY OF SPIRITUAL WISDOM

Also available
ATLANTIS
THE DRUIDS
CHRISTIAN ROSENKREUTZ
THE GODDESS
THE HOLY GRAIL

ALCHEMY

The Evolution of the Mysteries

selections from the work of
RUDOLF STEINER

Sophia Books

All translations revised by Christian von Arnim

Sophia Books
An imprint of Rudolf Steiner Press
Hillside House, The Square
Forest Row, East Sussex
RH18 5ES

www.rudolfsteinerpress.com

Published by Rudolf Steiner Press 2001

Series editor: Andrew Welburn
For earlier English publications of extracted material see p. 97

The material by Rudolf Steiner was originally published in German
in various volumes of the 'GA' (*Rudolf Steiner Gesamtausgabe* or
Collected Works) by Rudolf Steiner Verlag, Dornach. This
authorized edition is published by permission of the Rudolf Steiner
Nachlassverwaltung, Dornach (for further information see p. 102)

This edition translated © Rudolf Steiner Press 2001

A catalogue record for this book is available from the British Library

ISBN 1 85584 089 8

Cover illustration by Anne Stockton. Cover design by
Andrew Morgan
Typeset by DP Photosetting, Aylesbury, Bucks.
Printed and bound in Great Britain by Cromwell Press Limited,
Trowbridge, Wilts.

Contents

Introduction: Alchemy and the Rise of the Modern Mysteries

by Andrew J. Welburn

One thing has become, over the last few years in particular, ever more clear. For whether they are historians of science, or healers of the human psyche, or seekers of esoteric knowledge, all the researchers alike have had to acknowledge that alchemy is very far from having yielded up all its secrets.

Indeed in all these circles its fascination continues to grow, as new research reveals, for example, its relevance to some of the greatest pioneers of modern thought, such as Isaac Newton and the brilliant chemist Robert Boyle. Both these august figures have subsequently been laid claim to by mainstream science as its champions in what can now be seen as its rewriting of history, trying to present them as rationalist culture-heroes and materialist founding fathers. As more and more research has been done, however, the real complexities of the story could no longer be kept concealed, and a fascinating picture unfolds once more as it now emerges that these twin geniuses of the early Royal Society had really envisaged that their mathematical and physical discoveries should go hand in hand with a spiritual and esoteric science. Both of them devoted long hours to intense alchemical research. Boyle corresponded at length with the members of an international alchemical society, and believed himself to be drawing ever closer to discovering the ultimate *arcanum*. Moreover, their involvement cannot any longer be dismissed as a personal peculiarity, which we ought to leave behind among the shadows of their time. For it has become evident that this spiritual and occult side of their investigations often furnished them with the crucial concepts for their physical science. Newton most likely hit on his idea of gravity (contrary to the popular myth, it is unlikely that it hit *him* in the form of the apple from the tree) by meditating on mystical and apocalyptic symbols of universal order. Boyle's devastating critique of the chemistry of his day, we now know, was meant to clear the way for introducing the ideas of those 'adepts' in chemical wisdom with whom he believed himself to be in touch.[1]

In other ways too alchemy has invisibly become a part of the modern world. For example, the idea of great imaginative theatre, with powerfully depicted characters in interaction, first developed by Shakespeare and (in comedy) by Ben Jonson, is not only fundamentally indebted to alchemy on the level of references and allusions by the pioneers to the alchemy prevalent in their day. It owes to it something more essential, perhaps even the basic 'experimental' idea of letting different natures loose upon one another in an enclosed 'viewing place' (the 'chemical theatre' of the alembic), so as to let them change and be changed.[2] Earlier, medieval theatre had worked quite differently, reflecting the more fixed nature of society by retelling well-known tales, frequently with a didactic or religious emphasis, and in any case where the story was well known, e.g. from the Bible. Therefore it reinforced what people already knew, rather than keeping them on the edge of their seats wondering how a situation was going to turn out, and who would have to adapt.

The wider sense we have nowadays of human interactions as challenging, open-ended and full of potential, inviting us to find out as much about ourselves as about the other person, is in some large part an inheritance of the Shakespearean theatre, with what we now know to be its heady alchemy. The overwhelming tragic power of a King Lear is certainly the spectacle of modern, 'unaccommodated' humanity facing the terror and potential of an uncertain world in the storm, but the model for it is the creative violence of chemical reaction, of elemental transmutation. It is only a further reflection of this when modern depth-psychology rediscovers in the dynamic of character-formation the transformational processes of alchemy, realizing anew that we are philosophical stones needing to be urged into life, or that we cannot be thought of as existing enclosed and complete: we require the making-whole-through-the-other, the marriage of the king and queen, the *mysterium coniunctionis*.[3] In all these ways, even where they are no longer acknowledged by our culture, the deeper implications behind modern life are drawn frequently and often most profoundly from the cosmic and holistic vision of alchemical thought.

It would be a modern but very un-Shakespearian tragedy, therefore, if the underlying vision of the alchemical unity of life and cosmos were to be lost — even while we admit how much it has taught us. It would be to miss the very point of that alchemical unity to preserve the psychological analysis, or the awareness of alchemy's role in the history of science, and yet to keep all the separate roles clinically apart; this would be like the dissection which, as Goethe's positivist devil Mephisto gleefully remarks, can reveal everything about a living creature (except the unifying force of its spiritual life!). It is perhaps Rudolf Steiner's greatest contribution to the issue that he can explain not only the spiritual truth that lay behind the inspired ideas of alchemy, leading up to a Newton and a Boyle, but how it is also a part of the whole development of our consciousness up to the present — and into the future. It is quite inadequate, from his point of view, to see alchemy as a past stage of science, when people could still accept the role of the spirit — a 'paradisal' state which, as Jung seems to suppose, we may yearn nostalgically to regain, at least internally, psychologically. Rather than being held up in this nostalgic way, alchemy and the psychic 'individuation' process of the modern soul are for Steiner twin aspects of the same historic, evolutionary development. They are an intrinsic part, in fact, of the quest for knowledge concerning the workings of external substance and matter which led to modern science and to modern consciousness. And the whole process, for him, is far from over. The true story of alchemy is only starting to be told even by the new historians of the Newtonian scientific revolution. The true story of alchemy, though in a thoroughly scientific sense, is that of the rise of the modern Mysteries.

The alchemical quest begins, according to Steiner, with the

end of the ancient world and its integrated vision of the cosmos. In ancient civilization humanity still lived to a great extent in accord with the natural cycles — in fact they derived a deep spiritual satisfaction from the sense of harmonizing with their rhythms. Thus they felt God or the gods in everything; matter and spirit were one. But already in pre-Christian times human evolution was bringing a change in consciousness, as individuals started to develop a more separate sense of identity or personal destiny. The new consciousness offered a source of self-fulfilment to a kind of person who took more risks, made his own decisions and commitments. But its cost was the sense of oneness with the spirit in the cosmos. In modern times we have gone further and further down the road of individualistic consciousness, and experienced the alienation that goes with it.

If this were the whole picture, there would indeed remain nothing but nostalgia for our lost relationship to the cosmic whole. And many on both sides of the question try to tell us that this is the only picture we can have: the humanist that there is no going back on our independence because on it depends everything we have made of ourselves, our modern civilization, scientific thought, etc.; the psychologist that we have violated our natural relationship with the world, and so are caught in an insoluble contradiction. Christianity, according to Jung, fails to resolve the dilemma because it has not been able to penetrate the whole of the psyche, our unconscious, unreformed part.[4]

But for Steiner our present form of consciousness, or relationship to the world, is not an absolute break or violation in this way. It is a process that feeds back into the world, as we have discovered to be the case through the ecological crisis; when changing our relationship to the world, we have not left the world unchanged but altered its whole balance. We are part of an evolving, ever-changing relationship from which we cannot, in reality, ever divorce ourselves. The purely 'objective', 'outsider' consciousness sometimes claimed by science cannot really exist. Thus our connection with the rhythms of nature, for instance, has not actually been obliterated, to become the object of impossible nostalgia — it has simply shifted to other levels of interaction. The way we think about and manipulate nature clearly affects its entire rhythmic processes, as we insert ourselves into them in a completely different way. It need not be a negative situation — indeed it should be a creative one. Nor should it wrongly put the demands of knowledge and of religion (spirituality) at loggerheads. For from Steiner's point of view, when Christianity came to give spiritual significance to the seeking, developing individual, it also opened the way for a new quest to define our relationship to the cosmic forces, which had been radically transformed. The message of individual salvation was the outer, 'exoteric' content of Christianity; the other side of the relationship was expressed 'esoterically' in the rise of the modern Mysteries, bringing into consciousness our relationship to the creative forces around and beyond us. Of these Mysteries, the alchemical quest is a highly significant part.

In place of the either/or of the conventional scientific view, alchemy puts that very reciprocality, the interaction of

subject and object, which the ecological crisis in our relationship to nature has shown to be 'scientifically' necessary.
In his later presentations, Steiner returned in particular to the
alchemical triad of sulphur, mercury and salt, which
expresses this dynamic polarity and inner equilibrium.[5]

On the inner level, it embodies our ability to balance the
forces of involvement (expansion into, merging with: called
alchemically *sulphur*) and definition (contraction, crystallization: called alchemically *salt*). Psychologically, the bal-
ancing, whole-making power between them (called
alchemically *mercury*) is experienced as our true ego. But just
as important is the cognitive significance of the triad as a
model, overall, of the way we can insert ourselves consciously into the balance of nature. Instead of dragging us
back to a dependence upon nature's rhythms, alchemy
consciously understood in this way gives us creative freedom. Steiner's view of alchemy's trajectory into modern
thought surely also makes much better sense of the professed
Christian views and symbolism of the alchemical tradition as
a whole — even while he shares many of the insights of Jung
into the Janus-faced nature of the spiritual situation that has
come about. The answer is certainly not to lament the failure
of Christianity, but rather to see that the 'esoteric', Mystery-
dimension implicit in Christianity is an essential aspect of
the role Christianity is called upon to play in the con-
temporary world.

In developing those spiritual-scientific ideas or 'anthroposophy', therefore, whose relevance to our modern pre-
dicament is only becoming more clear as the new

millennium begins, Rudolf Steiner was able to draw upon the concepts of alchemical thought without being in any way 'backward looking' or unscientific. Indeed we have seen that he was being true to the deeper perceptions of those who had pioneered the scientific revolution itself, such as Newton and Robert Boyle, and, one might also say, to the latest 'anthropic' implications which have emerged within modern cosmology. These have reminded us that we can never be mere onlookers, that the first thing we know about the universe is that it is such as to produce ourselves as knowers.[6] The alchemical principle of seeking in the human knower (the microcosm) the key to the forces in the universe (the macrocosm) is thus by no means out of date. The spiritual implications of it are at the heart of the renewed Mysteries, in the shape of the spiritual-scientific alchemy which would deal with the inner side of our modern experience of nature.

In the lectures chosen to end this little introductory volume, Rudolf Steiner turns to that spiritual dimension above all. Alchemy has always been known in its higher manifestations as a way to contact the deeper levels of reality, described as the superhuman 'spirits' or guiding archangels of the universe. The principle of human freedom expressed in the modern Mysteries is in no way compromised by putting us in touch with these deeper 'intelligences'. The image of the archangel Michael fighting the dragon is itself a symbol of the attainment of inner freedom. As such it was central to Rudolf Steiner's thinking over much of his career, but especially so in his later years when he spoke increasingly about the importance of the 'Michael

Mystery'. This Mystery belongs particularly to certain times in human development, of which our own age is one. The freedom of the individual seeker for knowledge finds in it a special meaning, connected with mankind's role in the balance of cosmic evolution. It is the deeper significance of the individualism of human development. Having broken free, we are able to enter in a different way into relationship with the ruling cosmic powers. For this we need the knowledge of the modern Mysteries, and alchemy is finally seen in Rudolf Steiner's presentation as a step towards the cosmic understanding we will need for our future role. It is the path of inner freedom, and inner transformation — as it becomes cosmic reality it is also the way of Michael.

1. Alchemy and the Rise of the Modern Mysteries

Rather than seeing alchemy, as do so many, as an archaic vision – one which we have left behind, or to which we long to return – Rudolf Steiner locates the origins of alchemy at the genesis of the modern consciousness. It arose precisely when the ancient sense of the divine filling all things was fading away. Human beings now confronted a world of lifeless matter: God had disappeared, 'absconded' as the alchemists said. He could be found again, but only through a search and a struggle for knowledge, by penetrating once more into the hidden depths of the world. In the process, human beings discovered also much about themselves, the potential and the pathos of the human condition, human aspiration, the doubts and uncertainties and the search for God. In medieval times these elements formed the basis of the Faustian myth. Rudolf Steiner shows us how we can restore the whole picture of humanity's evolution up to the present – not rejecting the gains in material knowledge, but revealing that alchemy is the hidden, other side of the consciousness which has brought them within our grasp. It was a principle of Rudolf Steiner's philosophy that all knowledge transforms the knower. Restoring that principle to the understanding of science is the modern basis of his appreciation of alchemical thought. The recovery of the full dimension of modern consciousness lies at the heart of his 'anthroposophical' approach to the wisdom of alchemy.

The loss of the divine and the alchemical quest

For people of ancient times, the phenomena and processes of nature were nothing less than deeds of the gods.[7] They would as little have thought of treating a phenomenon of nature as an isolated event as we should think of considering a movement of the human eyes as a thing in itself and not as a revelation of the human soul and spirit. Natural phenomena were considered to be expressions of the gods, who manifested themselves through them. For the ancients, the earth's surface was as truly the skin of the divine earth being as our skin is the skin of an ensouled human being. We really have not the least understanding of the mood of soul of the people of antiquity unless we know that they referred to the earth as a body of the gods and to the other planets in our planetary system as brothers and sisters of the earth.

But then this direct relation to the things and processes of nature, which saw in the single object or phenomenon the revelation of the divine principle, changed into a totally different one. The divine part of natural phenomena disappeared. Suppose it happened to one of you that people saw you merely as a body in the same way that we see the earth — neutral and soulless. It would be absolutely horrible!

But this horrible thing really happened in the context of modern knowledge. And medieval scholars felt the horror of it, for from the standpoint of modern knowledge it is as though the divine principle has withdrawn from natural phenomena. Whereas in ancient times the objects and processes of nature were revelations of the divine world, this was followed by an intermediary period when the phenomena of nature were only pictures, no longer revelations, but only pictures of divine manifestation.

Ancient times: natural objects and processes, revelations of a divine world.
Medieval times: natural objects and processes, pictures of a divine world.

However, a modern person does not really have any idea of the way in which natural processes are pictures of a divine world. Let me give you an example that anyone can understand who knows a smattering of chemistry; it will show you what sort of conception of science the people had who at least still held the view that natural objects and processes are pictures of a divine world.

Do a simple experiment which is constantly being performed by chemists today. Take a retort and put into it oxalic acid, which you can get from clover, and mix this oxalic acid with an equal part of glycerine. Then you heat the mixture and carbon dioxide will be given off. When the carbon dioxide has evaporated, what remains behind is formic acid. The oxalic acid is transformed by the loss of carbon dioxide into formic acid. This experiment can easily be done in a laboratory and you can look at it as a modern chemist does, namely, as a complete and finished process. Not so a person in the Middle Ages before the thirteenth and fourteenth centuries. He looked at two different things. He said oxalic acid is found especially in clover but it occurs in certain amounts in the whole of the human organism, in particular in the part of the organism comprising the digestive organs — spleen, liver, and so on. In the area of the digestive tract you have to anticipate processes that are under the influence of oxalic acid.

Now it happens to be the case that oxalic acid, which plays a part in the human abdomen, is acted upon by the human organism itself in a way which is similar to the action of the glycerine in the retort. Here too we have a glycerine action. Now observe the remarkable result: under the influence of the activity of glycerine the transformed product of oxalic acid, namely, formic acid, passes into the lungs and the breath. And we breathe out carbon dioxide. We send out our breath and with it we send out carbon dioxide. Imagine the digestive tract instead of a retort and the lungs where the formic acid is collected, and higher up you have carbon dioxide in the air breathed out from the lungs. A human being, however, is not a retort! The retort simply demonstrates in a dead way what takes place in a human being in a living and feeling way. Thus, if a human being never produced oxalic acid in his digestive tract he would simply not be able to live. That is to say, his etheric body would have no sort of basis in his organism. If a human being did not change oxalic acid into formic acid, his astral body would have no basis in his organism. Human beings need oxalic acid for their etheric body and formic acid for their astral body. Or rather, it is not the substances they need but the inner activity going on in the oxalic acid process and the formic acid process. This is of course something which present-day physiologists have yet to discover; they still speak of what goes on in the human being as if these were external processes.

This was the first question put by the student of natural science in medieval times as he sat in front of his retort. He asked himself: 'Such is the external process which I observe; now what is the nature of the similar process in the human being?'

The second question was this: 'What is the same process like in the great world of nature outside?' In the case of the example I chose, he would have said: 'I look out over the earth and see the world of plants. Oxalic acid is present in a marked degree in wood sorrel and in all kinds of clover. But in reality oxalic acid is contained in all vegetation, even if it is sometimes in homoeopathic doses. There is a touch of it in everything. The ants find it even in decaying wood. The swarms of ants, which we human beings often find so troublesome, get hold of the oxalic acid which occurs all over the fields and meadows and is indeed found wherever there is vegetation, and change it into formic acid. We continually breathe in the formic acid out of the air, although in very small doses, and we are indebted to the work of the insects on the plants for changing the oxalic acid into formic acid.'

And the medieval student would say to himself: 'This metamorphosis of oxalic acid into formic acid takes place within us human beings and the same metamorphosis is present in the activity going on in nature.'

These two aspects presented themselves to the student with every process he carried out in his laboratory. There was, besides, something else that was very characteristic of the medieval student, something that has today been completely lost. Today we think, why, anyone can do research in a laboratory! It does not matter in the least whether he is a good or bad person. All the formulae are available; you only have to analyse or synthesize. Anyone can do it. However, in the days when nature was approached quite differently, when people saw in nature the working of divine forces both in humanity as well as in the natural world at large, then it was required of those who did research that they should at the same time have an inner piety. They must be ready to turn in soul and in spirit to the divine spiritual principle in the world. And it was a recognized fact that if a person prepared himself for his experiments as though for a sacred rite, if he were inwardly warmed in soul by the devout exercises he performed beforehand, then he would find that the experiments led him on the one hand inwards to an investigation of the human being, and on the other hand outwards to the examination of external nature. Inner purity and goodness were thus regarded as a preparation for research, and they regarded the answers they received to their questions posed by their laboratory experiments as being willingly given by divine spiritual beings.

This gives you a characteristic picture of the transition from the spirit of the ancient Mysteries to Mysteries such as were able to exist in the Middle Ages. A certain amount of the content of the ancient Mysteries still found a place in the medieval Mysteries as a kind of tradition. Nevertheless it was impossible in the Middle Ages to attain to the greatness and sublimity even of the Mysteries that survived comparatively late, such as those at Samothrace or Hibernia.[8]

What is called astrology has, of course, been preserved right up to our day in a traditional way, and the same applies to alchemy. But nothing is known today of the conditions necessary for a real knowledge of astrology or alchemy — in fact these conditions were hardly known any longer even in the twelfth and thirteenth centuries. It is quite impossible to arrive at astrology through reflection or empirical research. If such a thing had been suggested to those who were initiated in the ancient Mysteries, they would have replied: 'You have just as little hope of being successful in finding astrology through reflection and empirical research as you can have of discovering a person's secrets by those means if he does not tell you them.' Suppose there were a secret known to one person and no one else, and someone were to contend that they could find it out by experimentation or reflecting on it. That would of course be absurd. He could learn the secret only if it were told to him. And the ancients would have found it equally absurd to try and arrive at a knowledge of astrological matters by reflecting on them or doing experiments or undertaking observations. For they knew that it is the gods alone, or, as they were called later, the cosmic intelligences, who knew the secrets of the stellar worlds. They knew them, and they alone could tell them to human beings.[9] That is why human beings have to pursue the path of knowledge that leads them to a good understanding of and relationship with the cosmic intelligences.

A true and genuine astrology depends on a person's

ability to understand the cosmic intelligences. And what about true alchemy? That does not come from doing research in the manner of chemists today but from being able to perceive the nature spirits within the processes of nature and on being able to come to an understanding with them so that they tell you how the processes take place and what really happens. In those ancient times astrology was no spinning of theories or fancies, neither was it mere research through

The cosmic forces, here represented as the principles of the planets, can still be found, though deeply hidden, within the heart of matter. From J.D. Mylius, Philosophia reformata *(1622).*

observation; it was a conversation with the cosmic intelligences. And alchemy, too, was a conversation with nature spirits. This is the first thing you have to know. If you had approached an Egyptian of ancient times or particularly a Babylonian, he would have told you: 'I have my observatory for the purpose of holding conversations with the cosmic intelligences; I hold conversations with them by means of my instruments, for my spirit is able to speak with the help of my instruments.' And the pious medieval natural scientist who stood in front of his retort, investigating on the one hand the activity inside the human being and on the other hand the activity of nature as a whole, would have told you: 'I do experiments because through experiments nature spirits speak to me.' The alchemist was the person who conjured up nature spirits. What was regarded as alchemy in later times was nothing more than a decadent product.

The whole of ancient astrology owed its origin to conversation with the cosmic intelligences. But by the time of the first centuries after the rise of Christianity, ancient astrology, that is to say, conversation with cosmic intelligences, was a thing of the past. The tradition was still there. When the stars stood in opposition or in conjunction, and so on, then calculations were made accordingly. People still possessed everything which existed by way of tradition from the times when the astrologer conversed with cosmic intelligences. But although astrology was already over by this time, a few centuries after the founding of Christianity, alchemy still remained. Conversation with the nature spirits was still possible in these later times. And if we look into a Rosicrucian alchemical laboratory in the Middle Ages, let us say in the fourteenth or fifteenth century, we find instruments not unlike those of the present day; at any rate one can gain some idea of them from the instruments in use today. But when we look with spiritual vision into those Rosicrucian Mysteries, we find everywhere the earnest and deeply tragic personality of whom Faust is a later and indeed lesser development, particularly Goethe's Faust.[10] For in comparison with the scholar in the Rosicrucian laboratory with his deeply tragic countenance who can really no longer cope with life, Goethe's Faust is something like a newspaper picture of the Apollo Belvedere as compared with the real Apollo when he appeared at the altar of the Kabeiroi, taking form in the clouds of sacrificial smoke.

That is how it is. When one looks into these alchemical laboratories of the eighth, ninth, tenth, eleventh, twelfth and thirteenth centuries one is confronted with a very deep tragedy. This tragic mood, which characterized the most earnest people of the Middle Ages, is not properly recorded in history books, for the writers of those books have not looked into the depths of the human soul.

But the genuine scholars, who experimented with retorts to learn about the real nature of the human being and the cosmos, were none other in the early Middle Ages than magnified Faustian characters. They were all deeply conscious of one thing. They could all say: 'When we experiment, nature spirits speak to us: the spirits of the earth, the spirits of the water, the spirits of fire and the spirits of the air. We hear their whispered murmuring, the coming and going of their voices growing into harmonies and melodies and retreating again. Melodies resound when nature processes take place.' These scholars stood over their retorts and with a devout heart steeped themselves in the process that was taking place. For example, when they asked a question in the process of the transformation of oxalic acid into formic acid, the nature spirit gave answer so that they could make use of the nature spirit to discover what was going on in the human being. First of all the retort began to speak in colour. They perceived the nature spirits of the earth and the nature spirits of the water rising up out of the oxalic acid and asserting themselves, but then the whole apparition changed into the humming sounds of melodies and harmonies growing and retreating back into itself again. Such was their experience of the process that results in formic acid and carbon dioxide.

And if one could enter into the life of such a transition from colour to sound, then one could also enter with a deep and living knowledge into what the process could tell one about nature as a whole and about the human being. The scholar arrived at the feeling that the things and processes of nature revealed something more, something spoken by the gods, for they were images of divine existence. And such knowledge could be used for the benefit of human beings. Throughout these times, the knowledge of healing was closely and intimately bound up with an understanding of the world view of this age in general.

Now let us imagine we had the task of developing a therapy based on such perceptions. We have a human being in front of us. The same complex of external symptoms can of course be an expression of a whole variety of illnesses and their causes. However, with the method arising from this kind of knowledge — which is not to say that it can be done today in the same way as it was done in the Middle Ages, for today of course it has to be done quite differently — we would be able to say that if a certain complex of symptoms occurs, then it shows that the human being is unable to transform enough oxalic acid into formic acid. He has become too weak in some way to do it. One possible remedy would be to give him formic acid in some form, to help him from outside if he himself cannot produce formic acid.

Now it might happen in the case of two or three people whom you have diagnosed as not being able to produce formic acid that you treat them with formic acid and it works quite satisfactorily. Then you get a person with a similar complaint to whom you give formic acid and it does not help at all. However, as soon as you give him oxalic acid it helps immediately. Why is this? Because the deficiency of forces is located somewhere else, namely, where the oxalic acid ought to be changed into formic acid. In such a case, if we were to think along the lines of a researcher of the Middle Ages, we should say: 'Yes, under certain circumstances the human organism, on being given formic acid, will reply: "I do not want it. I do not ask for it in the lung or anywhere like that, I do not need it brought into the breath and the circulation. I want to be treated in quite a different place, namely, in the region of the oxalic acid, for I myself want to change the oxalic acid into formic acid. I do not want the formic acid. I want to make it myself." '

This is how different the situation can be. Of course a great deal of swindling and stupidity has gone on under the name of alchemy, but for the genuine scholar who was worthy of the name the subject of his research was always the study of healthy human nature in close connection with human nature when in a sick state. And this led to nothing less than conversation with the nature spirits. The medieval scholar definitely felt: 'I am associating with nature spirits. There was a time when human beings associated with cosmic intelligences. That is barred to me.'

In fact, my dear friends, since the nature spirits, too, have withdrawn from human understanding, and the objects and processes of nature have become the abstractions they now appear to be to the physicists and chemists of today, the tragic mood which was there in the Middle Ages no longer arises. For it was the nature spirits, who themselves could just reach back that far, who awakened in the medieval scholar the yearning for the cosmic intelligences. These had been accessible to the ancients, but the medieval scholars could no longer find their way to them with the tools of knowledge at their disposal. They could only find their way to the nature spirits. The very fact that they did perceive the nature spirits and were able to draw them into the field of knowledge made it so tragic for them that they were not able to approach the cosmic intelligences by whom the nature spirits themselves were inspired. They perceived what the nature spirits knew, but they could not penetrate through them to the cosmic intelligences beyond. That was the mood of the time.

The real cause of this tragedy was that while the medieval alchemists still acquired knowledge from the nature spirits, they had lost touch with the knowledge of the cosmic intelligences. And this in turn was also the cause of the fact that they were unable to attain to a complete knowledge of the human being, although they were still able to divine where such knowledge was to be found. And when Faust says:

And here, poor fool, with all my lore,
I stand, no wiser than before.[11]

we may really take the words as reminiscent of the feeling that prevailed in many a laboratory of the Middle Ages. For ultimately it was the nature spirits who gave the laboratory scholars what they knew, but they could not give them real knowledge of the soul.

In our time, a great deal has been lost, even in the way of traditional knowledge, but it must be found again. The medieval scholars had also heard of reincarnation. However, when they were in their laboratories, the nature spirits were in the habit of speaking about all kinds of things relating to substances or giving descriptions of occurrences in the world, but they never spoke at all about repeated lives on earth; they took no interest in the subject at all.

So, my dear friends, I have presented you with some of the thoughts which gave rise to the fundamentally tragic mood of the medieval natural scientist. He is indeed a remarkable figure, this Rosicrucian scientist of the early Middle Ages, standing in his laboratory with his deeply serious and

The Rosicrucian alchemist in his laboratory, where he seeks to communicate with the cosmic Intelligences. From H. Khunrath, Amphitheatrum sapientiae eternae *(1609).*

sorrowful face, not sceptical of human understanding but filled with a profound uncertainty of heart, with no weakness of will but with the awareness: 'I have the will! But how am I to guide it so that it may take the path that leads to the cosmic intelligences?'

There were innumerable questions arising in the heart of the medieval natural scientist! The monologue at the beginning of *Faust*, with all that comes after it, is no more than a weak reflection of Faust's endless questioning and striving.

Mysteries of the metals

Let us take one region of the earth as an example and use it to show the kind of knowledge which human beings came to acquire in the most ancient of the Mysteries when they looked up to the sun. There were types of Mystery sanctuaries which were arranged with a specially prepared skylight, so that at certain times of the day people could look at the sun with its light diminished. It must be understood that the most important chamber in many an ancient sun Mystery centre was one with a skylight in the roof, the window of which was filled with some kind of material — not glass of our modern kind but a material through which the orb of the sun was seen as in dim twilight. The pupil was then prepared to observe the solar orb in the right inner mood of soul. He had to make his feeling mind so receptive and perceptive that when, by way of the eye, he opened his soul to the sun with its dimmed-down light, it made a strong and lasting impression on him.

Of course many people look at the sun nowadays through smoked glass, but their perceptive faculty has not been tuned to take the impression into their souls so powerfully that it remains with them as a very special impression. The impression of the dimmed orb of the sun received by the pupils of these Mysteries after they had undergone exercises for a long time was a quite specific one. And anyone who, as a pupil of the Mysteries, was able to have this impression, could truly never forget it. It also increased his understanding of certain things. Then, after the pupil had been prepared by the majestic impression made upon him by the sun, he was led to experience the special quality of the substance of gold; and through this sun preparation the pupil actually came to a deep understanding of the quality of gold.

If you look into these things, it is painful to realize the trivial nature of the descriptions given in modern history books of why one or another ancient philosopher allocated gold to the sun or gave the same symbol to gold as to the sun. People no longer have any idea that what was known about this in ancient times proceeded in reality from long exercise and preparation. A pupil who looked with his whole soul into the dimmed light of the sun was being prepared to understand the gold of the earth.

And in what way did he understand it? His attention now awoke to the fact that gold is not receptive to that element which is normally the breath of life for organisms, and to which most other metals are thoroughly receptive, namely, oxygen. Oxygen does not affect or alter gold. This nonreceptivity, this obstinacy of gold with regard to the element through which human beings receive life, made a deep impression on the pupil of the ancient Mysteries. He realized that gold cannot approach life directly. Now neither can the sun approach life directly, and the pupil learnt that it is well that neither gold nor the sun can directly approach life. For he was gradually led to realize that because gold has no relationship with oxygen, the breath of life, it has a quite specific effect when it is introduced in a certain dosage into the human organism. It has no relation to the etheric body, no relation to the astral body directly, but it has a direct relation to the quality of thinking.

Just take a look at the extent to which thinking is removed from life, especially in our modern age! A person can sit like a sack of potatoes and think abstractly with great vigour. On the other hand, he cannot bring about any change in his organism merely by thinking; human thought has become more and more powerless. However, this thinking is set in motion by the ego organization, and gold introduced in the right dosage into the human organism can bring back power to thought. It restores to the life of thought the power to work down into the astral body and even into the etheric body; thus gold enlivens the human being by way of his thinking.

One of the secrets of these ancient Mysteries was the secret of gold in connection with the sun. The relationship between the substance gold and the cosmic working of the sun made a particular impression on the pupils of these ancient Mysteries. In a similar way the pupil was led to experience the working of the polar opposite of gold. Gold is an impulse for the quickening of human thinking, so that human thought can work down as far as the etheric body. And what would be the polar opposite to this?

The members of the human organism are the ego organization, astral body, etheric body and physical body, and gold enables the ego structure to work down into the etheric body. The etheric body can then work on the physical body, but gold makes it possible for a person to hold his thoughts in all their power as far as in the etheric body.

What is the polar opposite of this? It is an activity that manifests itself when something attracts the breath of life — oxygen — to itself either in a human being or in nature. And just as gold is unresponsive where oxygen is concerned and repels it, and therefore has no direct influence on the etheric or the astral body but only on the thought world of the ego structure, carbon has a direct affinity to the oxygen in the human being. As you know, we breathe out carbon dioxide. We make it by combining carbon with oxygen. And the plants require carbon dioxide in order to live. Carbon has the exact opposite properties to gold.

Carbon played an important role in the oldest Mysteries. In one direction they spoke of gold as a particularly important substance in the study of the human being, and in the other direction they referred to carbon. In these most ancient of Mysteries they called carbon the 'philosophers' stone'. Gold and the philosophers' stone were very important things in those ancient times.

Carbon appears on earth in a variety of forms. Diamond is carbon, a very hard form of carbon. Graphite is carbon. Coal is carbon. Anthracite is carbon. Carbon appears in the most diverse forms. However, by means of the methods that were customary in the ancient Mysteries, human beings came to understand that there exist still other forms of carbon besides those we find here on earth. And in this connection the pupil in the Mysteries had to undergo another preparation. For besides the sun preparation, which I have already told you about, there was also a moon preparation.

Added to the ancient sanctuaries of the sun Mysteries, we find a kind of observatory in which a human being could open his soul and his physical vision to the forms of the moon. Whereas in the sun training the pupil had to look at the sun at certain times of day in a diminished light, in moon training he had to expose his eyes to the different forms that the orb of the moon assumes by night for weeks at a time. Gazing thus with his whole soul, the pupil received a definite inner impression which gave him fresh knowledge. Just as the human being became capable of understanding the sun by exposing his soul to it, similarly, by exposing himself to the phases of the moon, the human being became capable of understanding the moon. He learnt the metamorphoses which the substance of carbon can undergo. On the earth carbon is coal or graphite, diamond or anthracite, but on the moon this substance is silver. And that was the secret of the ancient Mysteries: carbon is silver on the moon.[12] Carbon is the philosophers' stone, and on the moon it is silver.

The knowledge that was impressed so profoundly on the pupil in the ancient Mysteries was this: any substance whatsoever is only what it appears to be in a given place at a given time. It was sheer ignorance not to know that carbon is coal, diamond or anthracite only on the earth, and that what exists on the earth as diamond or graphite is silver on the moon. If we could at this moment dispatch a piece of ordinary black coal to the moon, it would be silver there. A vision of this radical metamorphosis was what the pupil attained in those ancient times. It is the foundation not of that fraudulent alchemy of which one hears today but of true alchemy.

Such ancient alchemy cannot be acquired by the abstract means of acquiring knowledge which we have today. Nowadays we observe things or we think about them. Alchemy could not be attained in that way at all. Nowadays a scientist directs his telescope to a certain star, determines parallel axes and the like and does calculation on calculation; or if he wants to discover what a particular substance is he uses a spectroscope, and so on. But everything that can be discovered in this way is infinitely abstract compared with what could once be learnt from the stars! And this ancient wisdom, this true astrology, could only be learnt, as I said yesterday, by establishing a living exchange with the intelligences of the cosmos.

When a human being was able to converse in his soul, in his spirit, with the intelligences of the cosmos, that in itself was the attainment of knowledge. The significance which *aurum* (gold) has for the human organism is connected with the secret of the sun; and through exposing his soul to the being of the sun, a human being entered into a relationship with the intelligences of the sun. It was these beings who

The metals as planetary principles. Meaning much more than common 'gold', the alchemical **aurum** *is a potency spread through the universe like the energy of the sun (sol), with many manifestations both visible and invisible. Inwardly, it is still experienced on a higher level while our earthly consciousness sleeps and the outer light disappears.*

could tell him of the properties of *aurum*. Similarly, human beings entered into a relationship with the intelligences of the moon.

Indeed, human beings came to understand these intelligences of the moon as those beings who were themselves once in ancient times the great teachers of humanity on earth when the primeval wisdom was taught on earth. They were the same beings who today send their forces and impulses down from the moon. They withdrew from the earth at a certain time in evolution, and there in the moon they founded a colony after the moon had separated from the earth. Thus those intelligences who once lived on the earth and are today the moon intelligences are connected with this secret, the secret of carbon-silver. Such was the character of knowledge in ancient times.

Let me quote another example. Just as the pupil could receive impressions from the sun and moon, so by means of still further preparation of soul he could also receive impressions from the other planets; and one of the secrets thus obtained was the one relating to Venus. Venus is studied today through a telescope and is regarded as being like any other star or planet. Just as the human body might be studied by investigating a section of the liver followed by a section of the brain, for example, simply investigating their cell structure as though they were not two radically different substances, in the same way a student will direct his telescope to Mercury, Venus and Mars and so on, believing all of them to be composed of similar substances. In ancient times they knew that if human beings were studying the moon or the sun, they could do that by means of what was directly related to the physical earth—the elements of earth, water, air and fire. If they extended their observation in a spiritual way to the moon, they came to the ether.

If, however, they extended their observation to Venus they came to a spiritual world, a purely astral world. What we see physically as Venus is only the external emblem of something that lives and has its being in the astral element, the astral light. Where Venus is concerned, physical light is something entirely different from physical sunlight. Physical sunlight still has a relationship with what can live on earth as earth-produced light, whereas Venus light—and it is childish to think of it simply as reflected sunlight—shines forth from the spiritual world. If the pupil exposed his soul to this light, he came to know which intelligences were connected with Venus. These are intelligences who live in continual opposition to the intelligences of the sun, and a great role was played in the ancient Mysteries by this opposition between the intelligences of Venus and the intelligences of the sun. People spoke with a certain justification of a continual battle between them. There were starting-points for such conflicts when the Venus intelligences began attacking the sun intelligences. There were times of intensified conflict, there were climaxes, catastrophes and crises. And in the circumstances of an attack and a catastrophe or crisis you had a section of that great battle of opposing forces which took place in the spiritual world, and appears in an external form only in the astrological and astronomical relationships between Venus and the sun. This battle took place in suc-

The metals as planetary principles. The moon (luna) is not so much common silver as the dissolving ('fiery') liquid of the alchemical transmutation, releasing consciousness from the limitations of the body; Mercury (quicksilver) is in its wider significance the power of balance or resolution on a higher level, guiding consciousness to knowledge on a higher plane. From an alchemical manuscript in the Vatican Library.

cessive phases. And no one can understand what lives on earth in the inner impulses of history if they do not know of this conflict between Venus and the sun. For all that takes place here on earth in the way of conflict, and everything else that happens in the evolution of civilization, is an earthly image of the conflict between Venus and the sun.

Such knowledge existed in the ancient Mysteries because there was a relationship between the human beings on the earth and the intelligences of the cosmos. Then came the epoch of which I have spoken, the epoch from the tenth to the fifteenth centuries AD. As the result of human evolution, the medieval researchers in their alchemical laboratories were no longer able to reach up to the cosmic intelligences, though they could still reach the nature spirits. They made numerous experiments — of which I gave you an instance in the last lecture, when I spoke of the transformation of oxalic acid into formic acid — which revealed to them the presence and activity of the gods in the processes and objects of nature. But they could do so only when they had prepared themselves fittingly through that spirit of reverence which I described as necessary to converse with the nature spirits. Now let us look more closely at the actual situation of such a researcher.

He stood in his laboratory and he told himself: 'I bring substances, retorts and ovens into my laboratory and I do various experiments. I ask nature certain questions by means of my experiments, and when I do this the nature spirits enter my laboratory with their revelations. I can perceive them.' This continued right up to the fifteenth century that nature spirits approached a Rosicrucian researcher who was properly prepared. However, he still knew theoretically that in ancient times researchers had not merely been able to reach the nature spirits but could come into contact with the higher cosmic intelligences who spoke to them of the secret of gold connected with the sun, the secret of silver and of carbon connected with the moon, and of the historically important secret of Venus, and so on.

It is true that they had records preserved by way of tradition telling them how there had once been this knowledge, but the records were not especially important to them. If one has once been touched by the spirit, then historical documents are not so terribly important as they are for our modern materialistic age. It is really astounding to see how infinitely important it is to many people when some discovery is made such as the recent case of the skeleton of a dinosaur found in the Gobi desert. Of course it is an important find, but such discoveries are never anything but individual broken fragments, whereas in a spiritual way we can really enter into the secrets of the cosmos. Historical documents were certainly not likely to impress those medieval investigators. The medieval alchemists used different means to acquire knowledge of how human beings had once been able to attain cosmic knowledge, while they could reach only the nature spirits behind the elements of air, fire and water. It was like this: in moments when certain observations of nature were being made or certain experiments being performed, and the researchers approached the sphere of the nature spirits, some of these spirits told them that there had once been human beings who had a connection with the cosmic intelligences. That was the pain which gnawed at the hearts of these medieval researchers, that the nature spirits spoke of a former age when human beings had had a connection with the intelligences of the cosmos. And the investigators had to conclude: 'These nature spirits can still tell us of a past age which has vanished into the unfathomable depths of human knowledge and human existence.' Thus this ability of the medieval alchemists to reach the nature spirits was really fraught with difficulty. On the one hand they approached the spirits of nature, the spirits of air and water; they approached gnomes, sylphs and undines in their living reality. On the other hand there were some among these beings who told them of things that overwhelmed them with despair, telling them how humanity had once been in connection not only with the nature spirits but also with the intelligences of the cosmos, with whom the nature spirits were still connected but whom human beings could no longer reach. That was the feeling of the medieval alchemists, and it often came to expression in a far more sublime, a far more grandiose and tragic manner than we find in Goethe's *Faust* (beautiful and powerful though this is!). The utterance that Faust addresses to the moon, to the shining silver moonlight in which he longs to bathe, would have been made with much greater depth by the scientists between the tenth and fifteenth centuries when the nature spirits told them about the secret of carbon and silver, a silver which is also closely and intimately connected with the human being. For what was it that these people of ancient times experienced alongside those communications? They experienced not only that *aurum* is connected with the sun but how *aurum* works in the human being, how *argentum* (silver) and carbon work in human beings and, similarly, how other metals related to the other planets work in the human being. In ancient times, people experienced these things in the circulation of the blood in their body. They experienced them in a conscious way. They felt the blood streaming and pulsing through their head and at the same time they felt it as an image of the whole earth. And that part where the head is not enclosed by bone, where it opens downwards towards the heart and the chest, they felt to be an image of what rises up from the earth into the atmosphere.

Thus what human beings learnt from the cosmos allowed the alchemist to recognize the metamorphoses that went on in his own organism; he could follow a planet in its passage through all his organs. We find here a confirmation of the penetrating words of Mephistopheles where he says: 'Blood is a very special fluid.'[13] For in its own metamorphosis our blood reflects those wonderful metamorphoses from carbon to silver. All of this is also active in the human blood.

The medieval scientist therefore regarded the loss of knowledge about the cosmic intelligences as a loss of his own humanity. And it is in reality just a faint reflection of this experience that we find in Faust when he opens the Book of the Macrocosm and endeavours to rise to the cosmic intelligences, then shuts the book again because he is unable to do so, and contents himself with the Spirit of the Earth. We have here only a faint echo of the dreadfully tragic mood we find in these medieval scientists, whose names have not even been passed down to us, when, on entering the sphere of the nature spirits through their alchemical investigations, they heard how human beings had once had a connection with the cosmic intelligences.

The standpoint of human wisdom (anthroposophy) today

I have spoken about the form, substance and metallic characteristics of the mineral kingdom in so far as they are related to the different levels of consciousness in human beings. Before extending my observations to include certain other metallic substances, I must make my position perfectly clear.

From what I have said, it could easily be inferred that I was recommending the ingestion of these substances in the form of nutriments as a means of inducing states of consciousness that differ from the normal. When discussing methods of achieving spiritual insight through inner training and discipline, one often hears the remark: 'I would be only too glad to know something of other worlds and other states of consciousness, but it is too difficult to carry out the exercises which are recommended; they take up so much time.'

A little later, perhaps, the people who make such remarks might start on these exercises. Then, after a time, the immediate demands of life intervene and they find they are unwilling to sacrifice their ingrained habits. By degrees they lose enthusiasm and the exercises are quietly dropped. Not surprisingly, these people achieve nothing; they find the need to practise spiritual exercises excessively irksome.

When they hear, for example, that the qualities of certain metals are associated with other levels of consciousness, they feel more reassured. If a small dosage of copper is all that is required in order to preserve a spiritual link with another person after death, then why not take it, they conclude, if it enables them to develop a higher level of consciousness.

The idea becomes all the more attractive when they hear that the practice adopted in the ancient Mysteries was not so very dissimilar, though in those days, of course, it was only carried out under the continuous and closest supervision of the initiates. And when people are told of this, they wonder why these old practices are not revived. But they overlook the fact that in ancient times the whole physical structure of human beings was differently constituted. In those days, and even as late as ancient Mesopotamian times, they lacked our present intellectual characteristics. Thoughts were not self-generated as today, but came to them through inspiration. Just as we realize today that we do not create the red of the rose, but receive the impression of the rose from outside, so the people of ancient times were aware that thoughts were transmitted via external objects, they were 'inspired', breathed into them. The reason for this was to be found in the different constitution of the physical organism, including even the composition of the blood. Therefore it was possible to administer highly potentized doses of those metals I have spoken of—homoeopathic doses as we call them today—in order to assist people in carrying out their spiritual exercises.

Let us suppose that a human being in Mesopotamian times was prescribed highly potentized doses of copper. Before taking it — this was the general practice of the time — he was instructed to perform certain specific spiritual exercises. In such cases, years rather than days of training were required of him before the highly potentized copper could be administered. And because his physical constitution was different from ours, he learned through his training to retrace the reactions upon the upper part of the body of this finely distributed, highly potentized copper that was circulating in his blood-stream. When copper was administered after such careful training, he felt inwardly that his words took on added warmth, because he himself had generated warmth in his larynx and in the nerves leading from the larynx to the brain. He was able to react with such extreme sensitivity to what was taking place within him because his physical constitution was different. If one were to administer highly potentized copper in similar circumstances today, it would of course take effect, but it would provoke a laryngeal condition and nothing further.

It is important, therefore, to understand the difference between the physical constitution of human beings in those times and today. Then one will no longer be tempted to induce other states of consciousness by administering medicaments, something which was normal practice in ancient times and was still frequently practised in the Middle Ages.

In our time, the only valid method is for a person to have an inner perception of the nature, the essential being of copper and thus develop a sensitive response to the colour of burnished copper, to the behaviour of copper in copper sulphate solution. By concentrating and meditating upon this response, he will ensure that he reacts in the right way.

But, you will object, in my book *Knowledge of the Higher Worlds*[14] there is no mention of what preparatory steps should be undertaken in order to develop this response to copper. That is so. But the instructions are given in my book in principle, though copper is not specifically mentioned. A description is given of how one should enter into the being of crystals, plants, etc. and the preparatory exercises are set out. But of course there is no information on how to meditate on the nature of copper; a whole library (rather than a book) would be needed for that. Nor is it necessary, since instructions already exist — exercises to promote self-confidence, for example, and exercises in concentration upon some specific theme or object. Such exercises, in effect, already cover what I have just said about the nature of copper. Only that is given as a subject for meditation which refers to its metallic nature.

A meditation upon some specific theme such as 'wisdom radiates in the light' has a decisive influence upon the inner life, if carried out in earnest. The effect would be the same as if someone were to explore the nature of copper from all angles and to concentrate on its physical aspect. In the first instance, our approach is from the moral standpoint, in the second, from the physical and chemical standpoint. It is far better for the non-chemist to enter the spiritual world from the moral standpoint.

It is necessary, therefore, to see things in their proper

relationship, because it would be a mistake for people today to follow uncritically the methods of the ancient Mysteries in order to gain insight into the spiritual world. The right course for today is to replace the external, physical approach by a more moral and spiritual approach. With the development of the physical organism, the human being's whole relationship to nature has been transformed. The composition of the blood, tissue, fluids and our whole physical constitution are different today from those of the people of ancient Mesopotamian times. This cannot be proved by anatomical analysis. In the first place, the anatomist spends most of his time dissecting corpses. Recently a scientific congress raised a cry of alarm and clamoured for more corpses. Anatomists found there was a shortage of corpses for investigating the hidden secrets of life. But it would not be easy to procure Mesopotamian corpses in order to pursue these investigations! In the second place, the anatomist would find no answer to the hidden secrets of life with his crude technique; these must be explored by spiritual means. Since our physical body is differently constituted from that of the ancient peoples, one point must be clearly established. It is still possible today to dispense highly potentized substances, metal potencies, for example. What is the reason for this? The explanation is that we have a deeper insight into the real being of nature. If we really understand the nature of the human body, we know that its functioning is modified by the metals tin, copper, lead, and so forth. And I have shown how they modify, in the first instance, the state of our consciousness.

Today, however, we are aware that changes take place in the body even under normal circumstances. Let us assume, for example, that we experience a change in that region of the body which radiates, as I pointed out, the activity of copper. Any such change is reflected in a disorder of the digestive organs, in the metabolic and limb system, in a disorder of the organs predominantly associated with the metabolism, digestion and the assimilation of nutrients. Every such disorder in the human organism, which we call disease, is also associated with the evocation of a different state of consciousness. The full implication of this must be borne in mind.

Now what is the significance of organic disease? I have said previously that for the human being of today the normal condition of waking consciousness is focused on the heart. Other states of consciousness are associated with other organs, but they always remain in the subconscious. The region of the larynx, including the area extending from the larynx to the brain, lives continuously in a state of consciousness sequential to the normal state which I have described. The region where the digestive organs are located shares the same time-scale as the deceased after death. Human beings always participate in this state of consciousness. Everyone shares the after-death experiences of those they knew personally in life. But they experience them below the heart, not in the heart. Therefore they are unaware of this experience; it remains in the subconscious below the threshold of consciousness. When some complaints such as digestive disorders for example occur in that region where man is spiritually in touch with the dead, the consciousness below the heart centre is modified; it begins to operate too actively.

What then is the explanation for certain kinds of gastric disorder? From the physical angle, it is simply a label for the physician's diagnosis. Now the point of view presented here is in no way directed against a purely physical approach to medicine. I recognize and appreciate its value. As anthroposophists, we do not adopt the attitudes of the dilettante, the amateur or the charlatan who disparage or criticize conventional medicine. We fully accept its findings. When a person suffers from a gastric disorder, the symptoms can be diagnosed physically; but as a result of his gastric condition he is also more able to share in the life of the deceased immediately after death. Of course a physical diagnosis has to be made before therapeutic treatment can begin. From the spiritual standpoint we would say that such a person feels impelled to preserve the spiritual link with the souls he has known on earth after their death. But he is unable to enter into the consciousness that lies below the heart. He is unaware that he is in communion with the dead.

That is the spiritual aspect of such a complaint. Gastric disorders arise because a person is too much attached to the dead. Under such circumstances a person is dominated by the dead. We are strongly influenced by that world which, as I indicated in earlier statements, is so much more real than the physical world.

Let us imagine we have a balance in front of us. If the pointer is deflected, the zero reading is restored by loading the other scale-pan. The absence of balance in a person who has developed such abnormal sensitivity in this consciousness below the heart that he is too attached to the dead—although he is quite unconscious of this—is analogous to the scale-pan that is loaded on the one side. Equilibrium is restored by adding an equivalent load to the other side. Thus, if the consciousness below the heart is too active, the consciousness in the region of the larynx must be diminished; the heart lies between, it acts as a regulator and is the knife edge on which the beam of the balance oscillates. Equilibrium is restored by administering copper. I have elsewhere pointed out that a person's body today is constituted in such a way that the larynx reacts to copper. The metabolic and laryngeal systems are as closely related as the two sides of the balance. One may be adjusted by means of the other. If suitable doses of copper are administered, the patient is inclined to withdraw somewhat from the realm of the dead and his health improves, whereas otherwise he increasingly identifies with that realm.

That is the spiritual aspect of healing. Today we are aware that all substances have both a physical and moral aspect. The old initiates could make use of the physical aspect for the benefit of their pupils but only after their pupils had undergone extensive training. It should no longer be used in the same way today. Today the moral attributes are the province of mental development, the physical attributes that of the doctor. It is important that the person who is familiar with the physical side of substances and makes a detailed study of this aspect should also supplement his information by a knowledge of the moral side. This must be strictly adhered to as regards our perception today and with regard to practical perception in the field of spiritual methodology. The human organism has changed radically with the passage of time and the close relationship that used to exist between knowledge of the moral and physical aspects of substances has been lost and must now be restored again.

2. Alchemy and Consciousness: The Transmutation

Rudolf Steiner now takes us deep into the secrets of the alchemical process. The answers to the mysteries of substance actually lie within our own consciousness. As we uncover ever deeper levels of consciousness within us we are also discovering new dimensions, new aspects of our relationship to the cosmos. If we can gain the spiritual strength to overcome the standpoint of ordinary consciousness – the safe, ordinary perspective on things with all that it provides for us – we can transform our awareness and share in the reality of the starry worlds, the secrets of the past, and the life beyond death. We can discover at once the mysteries of the world and our own immortal self.

I should like to draw your attention to a peculiar phenomenon when we observe the world of stars on the one hand and the world of plants on the other. I should like to describe these things entirely from the point of view of inner experience, exactly as they occur in and are revealed to direct spiritual experience and investigation. My explanation will not be supported by any tradition, literary or otherwise. But first of all, I should like to point out a peculiarity that is familiar to anyone who explores spiritual aspects in the way I have described.

Let us visualize the following picture. Above us is the world of stars, below is the earth. The point from which we start our enquiry we call our point of observation. At the second level of consciousness, we are able to confirm that the archetypal forms are present in the cosmos, and that they are mirrored in the earth, not as reflected images but in the form of living plants. These plants do not appear as lifeless, unreal, nebulous images, but as concrete reflections created by the earth. One feels that the earth must be there to act as a mirror so that the plant beings in the cosmos can grow out of this terrestrial mirror.

Without the solid earth there could be no plants. And just as a mirror intercepts the light and acts as resistance—for otherwise it could not reflect—so the earth must act as a reflecting medium in order that the plants may come into being.

We can now pursue the matter further. When we develop such a second level of consciousness, a consciousness which works independently of sensory impressions, we can take the next step towards developing inner strength of soul, the spirit of love towards all created and living beings. The acquisition of these new powers is seldom recognized as a positive force for knowledge. If this power of love fills our heart and soul on entering into this realm that is so differently constituted, where the cosmos no longer appears bright with stars but is the abode of spiritual beings, if we can preserve our spiritual, mental and physical identity and extend the infinite power of love and devotion to all beings after embarking on what we might call the spiritual ocean of the universe, then we progressively perfect our knowledge and understanding. We then develop the capacity to perceive clairvoyantly not only the animal and plant kingdoms, but also the mineral kingdom and especially that part of the mineral kingdom which is crystalline in structure. For those who wish to investigate the higher worlds, mineral crystals offer an excellent field for observation and study.

Once we are fully familiar with the animal and plant kingdoms, we are then in a position to investigate the mineral world of crystals. And once again, we feel impelled to turn our attention from the mineral kingdom on earth to the contemplation of the cosmos. And again we find there a living reality, the archetypes similar to those of the plant kingdom. But the picture now presented to us is totally different. We become aware of a living reality in the cosmos; the mineral world of crystals that we see on earth is the creation of an active, spiritual principle in the cosmos. In its progressive descent to the earth, it is not reflected in the earth or by means of the earth. That is the crucial point. When we raise our consciousness from contemplation of the mineral kingdom of crystals to the cosmos and look back to earth again, the earth no longer acts as a mirror; it appears as if the earth has vanished from our sight. We can no longer say, as we said of the plants, that earth below us reflects the higher beings. On the contrary, the earth does not act as a reflecting medium; it has seemingly vanished.

When we have meditated upon the spiritual vista evoked by the mineral kingdom of crystals, when we direct our spiritual eye from cosmic space to the earth, we appear to be suspended over a terrifying abyss, over a void. We must remain in a waiting attitude. We must keep a firm hand on ourselves, we must preserve our presence of mind. The period of waiting should not be too prolonged, otherwise our fear is magnified; we are terrified because there is no ground under our feet. This sensation, which is wholly foreign to us, reduces us to a state of panic if we do not preserve our self-control, the necessary presence of mind which enables us to take active steps to see beyond this void.[15] For this reason we must look beyond the earth which is no longer present to our spiritual vision. Then we are obliged to contemplate, not only that aspect of the mineral kingdom that is associated with the cosmos, but also its relationship to the total environment. The earth ceases to exist for us. We must see the mineral kingdom as a totality.

We then experience a current of cosmic energy from below, in contrast to the cosmic energy of the plants which streams down from above. We see everywhere currents and counter-currents, converging currents of cosmic energy from all directions. In the case of the plants this stream of cosmic energy flows down from above, the earth offers resistance and the plants grow up out of the earth. In the case of the mineral kingdom we are aware that it is created through the free interplay of these cosmic currents. In the case of the mineral kingdom of crystals, nothing is reflected back from the earth. Everything is mirrored in its own element.

If you discover a quartz crystal in the mountains, it is usually found in a vertical position. Its base is embedded in the rock. This is due to the intervention of terrestrial, ahrimanic forces,[16] which act as a disruptive factor. In reality, the quartz is formed by the pressure of a spiritual element from all sides; there is an interplay of reflecting facets and you see the crystal free in cosmic space. Each single crystal, whose every facet is perfectly fashioned, is a little world in itself.

Now there are many types of crystal formation—cubes, octahedrons, tetrahedrons, rhomboids, dodecahedrons, monoclinics, triclinics, every conceivable kind of structure in fact. When we examine them, we note how the currents of cosmic energy converge and interact to form the quartz crystal, a hexagonal prism terminating in a hexagonal pyramid, or a salt crystal possibly in the shape of a cube, or a pyrites crystal in the shape of a dodecahedron. Each of these crystals is formed in the way I have described. And there are as many different cosmic forces, indeed as many worlds in cosmic space, as there are crystals in the earth. We begin to have insight into an infinitude of worlds.

As we look at the salt crystal, we realize that a spiritual principle is active in the universe. The salt crystal is a manifestation of that spiritual reality which permeates the whole universe; it is a world in itself. Then, from an examination of the dodecahedron, we discover that there exists in the universe something that permeates the world of space; the crystal is the manifestation of a whole world. We are looking at countless beings, each of which is a world in itself. As human beings here on earth, we conclude that the sphere of the earth is the focal point of the activities of many worlds. The thoughts and deeds of a diverse variety of beings are reflected in all that we think and do here on earth. The infinite variety of crystal forms reveals the multitude of beings whose activities culminate in the mathematical-spatial forms of the crystals. In the crystals we recognize the presence of the gods. As an expression of reverence, of adoration even towards the universe, it is far more important to allow the sublime secrets of this universe to possess our souls than to gather theoretical knowledge on a purely intellectual basis.

Anthroposophy should lead to this feeling of being at one with the universe. Through anthroposophy, human beings can perceive in every crystal the activity of a divine being. Then cosmic knowledge and understanding begin to fill a person's whole soul. The task of anthroposophy is not to appeal to the intellectual faculty alone, but to enlighten the whole person and show his total involvement in the universe; to inspire him with reverence and devotion towards it. Every object and every event in the world will be invested with a spirit of selfless service proceeding from the heart and soul of the human being. And this selfless service will be rewarded by knowledge and understanding.

When we are in contact with the cosmos and see the crystals emerging out of the manifestations of the mineral kingdom of the crystals, we feel a sense of satisfaction. But very soon that state of anxiety and fear which I have already mentioned returns again. Before discovering the divinely ordered world of crystals, we had been filled with fear. When we are aware of that divinely inspired world, this feeling of uncertainty vanishes; but after a time a strange sensation overtakes us and the fear returns, the feeling that the whole process of crystal formation is insubstantial and provides only partial support.

Let us take the example of the two kinds of crystal already mentioned, a salt crystal and a pyrites, a metallic crystal. Pyrites gives the impression that it can provide us with solid support, that it is firm and durable. The salt crystal, on the other hand, appears to offer no support; it seems insubstantial and we feel as if we might fall through it.

In brief, then, the fear that once possessed us, the fear that we are suspended over an abyss because the earth has become a void, has not finally been overcome in relation to certain forms. This sensation of fear has definite moral implications. At the moment that we feel a recurrence of this fear, we become aware not only of all our past sins, but also of those of which we are potentially capable.

All this acts upon us like a leaden weight that drags us down and threatens to plunge us into the abyss which the mineral crystals open up before us and which is ready to engulf us. At this point we must be prepared for an additional experience. We realize that the sum of our experiences demands of us courage and we confidently proclaim: 'I am firmly anchored, I cannot drift from my moorings; the centre of gravity of my own being now lies within myself.'

Never in the whole course of life do we need more confidence, more moral courage than at the moment when, confronted with the crystal world, the leaden weight of egotism — and egotism is always a sin — weighs upon the soul. The transparent void over which we are suspended now holds a terrible warning for us. If we stand firm and remain self-reliant, we can say: 'A spark of the divine is within me; I cannot perish, for I partake of the divine essence.' If this becomes a concrete experience and not mere theoretical belief, then we have the courage to be self-sufficient, to stand on our own feet. We are ready and determined to press on further.

We now learn something further about the mineral kingdom. So far we have heard about crystals belonging to the minerals. We have already discussed their external form; now we become aware of their composition and structure, their substance and metallic nature. And we discover how certain basic metals in their different ways act as a stabilizing factor. For the first time we begin to understand how human beings are related to the cosmos. We learn of the different characteristics of the metals, of the substance of the mineral nature and we really begin to feel in ourselves that centre of gravity which I have just mentioned.

In what I am about to say, I have no choice but to use terminology that describes the material world; it should not be understood simply in its literal meaning. When we speak of the heart or head, the common-sense view conjures up a picture of a physical heart or head. But they are, of course, spiritual in origin. And so when we look at man in his totality, as an entity consisting of body, soul and spirit, we have the clear impression that his centre of gravity lies in the heart. This centre guards him against extremes, prevents him from being the plaything of external circumstances and lends him stability. If we retain that courageous spirit which I have just mentioned, we shall ultimately find ourselves firmly anchored in the universe.

When a person loses consciousness he is not firmly anchored. If he suffers a psychological shock—for under these conditions he is more susceptible to pain than normal, and pain, after all, is an intensification of inner feeling—then he is not in a normal state of consciousness. Under conditions of pain normal consciousness no longer exists. Between birth and death human beings live in a kind of intermediate state of consciousness. This may well serve for the normal purposes of daily life. But if this consciousness becomes too weak, too tenuous, they lose consciousness. If it becomes too dense, too concentrated, pain ensues. The fainting loss of consciousness and the state of tension under the influence of pain are polarities which illustrate abnormal states of consciousness. This describes exactly our reactions to the world of mineral crystals before we become aware of their substance—on the one hand, the feeling that in a fainting state we might at any moment be dissolved in the universe, and on the other hand the feeling that under the influence of pain we might collapse. Then we feel that everything that provides stability is centred in the cardiac region. And if we have developed our consciousness to the level already indicated, we then perceive that everything that sustains our ordinary waking consciousness, all that keeps it 'normal', if I may use this somewhat crude expression, is gold, *aurum*, which is finely distributed over the earth and works with greater immediacy upon the heart than upon any other organ.

Previously we learnt about the formation, the crystallization of minerals. We now become aware of their substance, their metallic nature. We realize the manner in which this metallic nature works upon human beings themselves.

Outwardly we see the crystal formations of the metals in the mineral world. But we know inwardly that the forces of gold, which are finely distributed over the earth, sustain our heart and maintain the normal consciousness of our daily life. And so we can say, gold works upon the heart centre of man. On the basis of this information we are now in a position to start our investigations. If, taking the metal gold as we know it, we concentrate upon its colour, its hardness and all aspects of its composition and structure and then transform the experience into inner reality, we find that gold is related to the heart. By concentrating on other metals, on iron and its properties, for example, we discover what effect iron has upon us. Gold has a harmonizing influence, it resolves tension and conflict and human beings are thereby restored to a state of inner equilibrium. If, after becoming familiar with all its aspects, we concentrate intently on iron, forgetting the entire universe and concentrating solely upon the metal itself so that in a manner of speaking we inwardly merge with iron, become identified with it, then we feel as if our consciousness were rising upwards from the regions of the heart. We are still fully conscious as we follow our consciousness as it ascends from the heart to the larynx. If we have carried out our spiritual exercises adequately, no harm can result; otherwise a slight feeling of faintness overtakes us. As our consciousness ascends, we recognize this condition from the fact that we have developed an intense inner activity, a heightened consciousness. Then we gradually transpose ourselves into this ascending consciousness and encounter the world where we see the group soul of the animals.[17] By concentrating on the metallic nature of iron, we have now entered the astral world.

When we become acquainted with the form of the metals, we reach the realm of the higher spiritual beings; when we become acquainted with their substance and metallic nature, we enter the astral world, the world of souls. We feel our consciousness rising upward to the larynx and we emerge into a new sphere. We owe this shift of consciousness to our concentration upon iron and we feel that we are no longer the same person as before. If we attain this state in full, clear consciousness, we are aware of having transcended our former self; we have entered into the etheric world. The earth has vanished, it no longer holds any interest for us. We have ascended into the planetary spheres which have become our abode. Thus we gradually withdraw from the body and become integrated into the universe. The path from gold to iron is the path leading into the universe.

After gold and iron, we next concentrate upon tin, upon its metallic nature, its colour and substance, with the result that our consciousness becomes wholly identified with tin. We feel that our consciousness is now rising to still higher levels. But if we undertake this step without adequate preparation, we faint almost completely. Scarcely any sign of consciousness remains. If we have prepared ourselves in advance, we can hold ourselves in this state of diminished consciousness;

but we feel that our consciousness is withdrawing still further from the body and ultimately reaches the region between the eyes. Though the vast expanse of the universe encompasses us, we are still within the realm of stars. The earth, however, begins to appear as a distant star. And we conclude that we have left our body on earth, that we have ascended into the cosmos and share the life of the stars. All this is by no means as simple as it sounds. What I have described to you, what we experience when we follow the path of initiation, namely, that consciousness is situated in the larynx, the base of the skull or the forehead, is an indication that all these various states of consciousness are permanently present in human beings. All of you sitting here have within you these states of consciousness, but you are not aware of it. Why is this so? Human beings are complex beings. If at the moment when you were conscious of the whole laryngeal structure you could dispense with your brain and sense organs, you would never be free of this slight subconscious feeling of faintness. And this is what in effect happens; it is simply overlaid by the ordinary consciousness associated with the heart, the consciousness associated with gold. It is common to all of you, it is part of your human make-up. A part of you that shares this consciousness is situated in the stars and does not exist on earth at all.

The consciousness associated with tin lies further out in the cosmos. It would be untrue to state that the earth is your sole habitat. It is the heart that anchors your consciousness to the earth. That which has its centre in the larynx is out in the cosmos and, situated still further out, is that which has its centre in the forehead (tin). The consciousness associated with iron embraces the Mars sphere, tin the Jupiter sphere. Only in the consciousness associated with gold do you belong to the earth. You are always interwoven with the universe, but the consciousness associated with the heart conceals this from you.

If you meditate on lead or some similar metal and again concentrate on its substance and metallic nature, you relinquish the body completely. You are left in no doubt that your physical body and etheric body are left behind on earth. They appear strange and remote. They concern you as little as the stone concerns the rock on which it rests. Consciousness has left the body through the crown (the sagittal suture) of the head. Wherever we turn, a minute quantity, a tincture of lead is always to be found in the universe. This form of consciousness reaches far out into space; with the consciousness that is centred in the cranium, man always remains in a state of complete insensibility.

Picture the state of illusion in which people habitually live. When they are sitting at their desk making up their accounts or writing articles, they fondly imagine that they are thinking with their head. That is not the reality. It is not the head as such but its physical aspect that belongs to the earth. The head consciousness extends from the larynx upwards far out into the universe. The universe reveals itself solely in the head centre. What determines your human condition between birth and death is the heart centre. Whether you write good or bad articles, whether your accounts may or may not be to your neighbour's disadvantage—this is determined by the heart centre. It is pure illusion to imagine that a human being's head consciousness is confined to the earth alone, for, in effect, it is in a permanent state of oblivion. And that is why it is also peculiarly subject to pain from which other organs are free. Let me take this point a little further. When, in our present state, we try to find the reasons for this situation, we are continually threatened from the spirit with the annihilation of our intellectual consciousness, with a breakdown of our whole consciousness and a collapse into total oblivion.

Our picture of the human being is then as follows: in the larynx (iron) human beings develop the consciousness that reaches to the archetypes of the animal kingdom. It is the consciousness that belongs to the stars, but we are unaware of it in ordinary life. Higher still, in the region of the eyes (tin) is the consciousness of the archetypes of the plant kingdom and below are their reflected images. Crowning all is the centre of the lead consciousness which reaches to the Saturn sphere; our head centre is oblivious of the articles we write, they are the product of the heart centre. But the head is fully aware of the happenings in cosmic space. Our description of terrestrial events and activities proceeds from the heart; the head, meanwhile, can concentrate on the manner in which a divine being manifests himself in pyrites, in a crystal of salt or of quartz.

If the audience present here is surveyed with the consciousness associated with initiation, it is evident that you are listening to what I am saying with your hearts, whilst your three higher levels of consciousness are out in the cosmos. The cosmos is the scene of activities of an order wholly different from those known to ordinary earthly consciousness. The web of our destiny, our karma is woven for all of us in the cosmos, especially in what is enacted there and radiates far and wide.[18]

Thus we have gradually come to understand the human being through his relationship with the universe — how fundamentally he is associated with the external world, is continually under the threat of annihilation from without, of reduction to oblivion, and is ultimately sustained by the heart.

When we meditate on other kinds of metals our spiritual approach is different. We can follow the same procedure with copper as we have done with iron, tin and lead. When we meditate on the metallic nature of copper, we become merged, at one with it; our whole soul is permeated with copper, with its colour and consistency, its curiously ribbed surface. In brief, we become wholly identified in our mental response to the metallic nature of copper. Then we do not experience a gradual transition towards oblivion, but rather the reverse. We have the sensation that something floods our whole inner being; our response grows more sensitive. We have a definite impression that when we meditate on copper it pervades our whole being. It radiates from the centre below the heart and is diffused over the whole body.

It is as though we had a second body, a second person within us. We have a sensation of inner pressure. This sets up a slight pain that gradually increases. Everything seems to be in a state of inner tension.

When we invest this condition with the consciousness associated with initiation, we feel the presence of a 'second man' within us. And this experience has important implications, for we can say to ourselves: the normal self, the legacy of birth and education, the instrument through which we perceive the world, accompanies us through life; but through training and meditation we can come awake in this second man who now takes over his potential for perception. This second man is indeed a remarkable being. He does not possess separate eyes and ears, but is simultaneously eyes and ears together. He resembles a sense organ with delicate powers of perception; he perceives things that we do not normally perceive. Our world becomes suddenly enriched.

Just as a snake can slough its skin, so it is possible for a short time — and much can be experienced in the course of a few seconds — for this second man, the 'copper man', to withdraw from the body and move about freely in the spiritual world. He can be separated from the body, though at the cost of increasing pain. When we are dissociated from the body we have a wider range of experiences. When we have reached the point when we can relinquish the body, we are then able to follow a person who has passed through the gateway of death.

In that event all our terrestrial associations with the deceased are ended. The latter has been buried or cremated, he has severed his connection with the earth. When we relinquish the body with the second man, that is, with clairvoyant perception, we are able to follow the journey of the soul after death. And then we learn that the soul in the first years or decades after death relives in reverse order its life on earth. This is a fact that can be observed since we accompany the soul through the gateway of death. The time taken to recapitulate our life experiences is a third of our life span. A person who dies at 60 will recapitulate his life experiences over approximately 20 years. We can follow his soul throughout this period. We can now learn much about a person's experiences after death. In recapitulating his life, the experiences are of a different order.

Forgive me if I give a somewhat crude example. Let us assume that three years before your death you gave someone a box on the ear. You were annoyed with him and you exploded with anger; you caused him physical and moral pain. You derived a certain satisfaction from punishing him for having offended you. Now, when you recapitulate your life in reverse order and come upon this episode after a year, you do not experience your original outburst of anger, but the physical and moral pain of your victim. You live right into his feelings and experience mentally the box on the ear; you re-experience the pain you have inflicted. And the same applies to all actions. You experience them exactly as others who were involved experienced them. It is possible to follow a person's soul after death through all such experiences.

The ancient Mesopotamians who owed their cultural impulses to the Mystery teachings had deeper insight into these matters than people today. The remarkable fact is that in those days the ancient Mesopotamians actually lived in the consciousness associated with the larynx, whereas we today live in the consciousness associated with the heart. The consciousness natural to them was a kind of consciousness associated with iron; their experience was associated with the universe; for them the earth did not have the solid consistency it holds for us. When under particularly favourable conditions they lived, for example, in communion with the beings of Mars, there came a moment of time when beings came over from the moon and brought with them other beings such as those we perceive with the consciousness of the second person. And thus indirectly the Mesopotamians learned of sublime truths relating to life after death. They received their instruction in these truths from the external universe. This is no longer necessary for us today when we can follow the dead without intermediary help. We can follow them as they live through their experiences in reverse sequence and each experience in reverse. And the strange thing is that when we are identified with this second man we find ourselves in a world that is infinitely more real than the world of our phenomena. This present world and the sum of our experiences there appear insubstantial in comparison to the solid, exacting world of reality which we have now entered.

In accompanying the dead in the way described, we experience everything on a magnified scale; everything appears to be more intensely real. By comparison, our world of phenomena leaves a nebulous impression. To anyone who is linked with the world of the dead through the consciousness associated with initiation, the physical world appears like a painted masquerade and an initiate who, through meditation, has been closely associated with the dead in this way would say: 'You are all painted masks. There is no reality about you; you are simply painted masks sitting on your chairs.'

True reality is only found beyond the realm of physical existence. The fact is that the reality of this world is illusory in comparison with that sublime reality which is revealed to us when we follow a soul beyond the gateway of death. There the soul endures in a world that we can experience ourselves when we are identified with the second person who can relinquish the physical body, if only for a short time. But in that short space of time much can be experienced. The existence of this world, the frontiers of which border directly on those of the phenomenal world, is never in doubt. It is a world in which the deceased are living more abundantly. We apprehend them through this second man who relinquishes the physical body. We have suffered no loss of consciousness but our consciousness is, on the contrary, more deeply interfused.

If we rise above the heart centre, our consciousness becomes more dimmed, we are near to a state of unconsciousness. If we descend below the heart centre our consciousness is intensified. We enter a world of reality, but we must learn to bear the pain and suffering this entails. But if we breach the walls surrounding this world with courage and determination, our entry is assured.

We have now arrived at an understanding of ordinary everyday consciousness, of a second consciousness in the larynx, a third in the region of the eyes, a fourth that reaches out into the universe at the crown of the head, and a fifth that is unrelated to the worlds of space and leads us back into the world of time. We travel through time; when we attain this fifth level of consciousness we share the same time-scale in reverse as the deceased. We have stepped out of space into time.

Everything therefore depends upon our ability to transpose ourselves into different states of consciousness, which open up to us new worlds. On earth, a human being is the prisoner of a single, insulated world because he knows only one state of consciousness; in all other states of consciousness he is asleep. If we awaken them and develop them, we can experience the other worlds.

The secret of spiritual investigation is that human beings transform themselves through transmutation of their consciousness. We cannot penetrate into other worlds by adopting conventional methods of research and investigation; we must undergo metamorphosis, transform our consciousness into new and different forms.

3. Alchemy and Archangels

The deepest meaning of alchemy transcends our personal experience and makes us aware once more of the divine-spiritual at work behind nature. In these final studies, Rudolf Steiner explores some of the fundamental patterns, such as the triad of mercury-sulphur-salt, and their ultimate relationship to the spiritual-angelic powers. These were formerly understood in ways appropriate to the past, but Rudolf Steiner regards it as vital that we find new, modern understandings of what they mean for the present. Michael conquering the dragon, for instance, can be experienced in the change of the seasons, in the processes of nature, but is also an 'imagination' that can grow with us beyond nature-consciousness and lead to a spiritual reality – one that demands above all to be recognized in our own time and the future. Overcoming materialism does not mean rejecting it; it means restoring the wholeness of vision, physical and spiritual, which had been the goal of alchemy from the very beginning.

The alchemy of nature: mercury, sulphur, salt

Let us now look at this earth of ours. It has a solid core hidden below its visible outer surface, which in turn is largely covered with water, the hydrosphere. The continents are only floating in this great watery expanse. And we can picture the hydrosphere as extending up into the atmosphere, for the atmosphere is always permeated by a watery element. Certainly this is much thinner than the water of the sea and the rivers, but there is no definite boundary in the atmosphere where the watery element comes to an end. Hence if we are to show schematically what the earth is like in this respect we should have, first, a solid core in the centre.[19] Around it we have the watery regions. I must of course indicate the way the continents jut up; they will have to be exaggerated, for they should really be no more prominent than the irregularities on the skin of an orange. Then I must put in the hydrosphere, this watery part of the atmosphere all round the earth. Let us look at this picture and ask ourselves what it really represents. It is not something made up entirely out of itself; it is water shaped by the whole cosmos. This body of air and water is spherical because the cosmos extends round it as a sphere on all sides. And this means that strong forces play in on the earth as a whole.

The effect is that if we were to look at the earth from some other planet it would appear to us as a great water drop in the cosmos. There would be all sorts of prominences on it — the continents which would be rather differently coloured — but as a whole it would appear to us as a great water drop in the midst of the universe.

Let us now consider this from a cosmic standpoint. What is this great water drop? It is something which takes its shape from its whole cosmic environment.

If one approaches the matter from the perspective of spiritual science, bringing imagination and inspiration to bear on it, one learns what this water drop really is. It is nothing but a gigantic drop of quicksilver, but the quicksilver is present in an extraordinarily rarefied condition.

That such high rarefactions are possible has been demonstrated by the work of Frau Dr Kolisko. At our Biological Institute in Stuttgart the attempt has been made for the first time to put this on a scientific basis. It has been possible to make dilutions of substances up to one part per trillion, in fact to establish precisely the effects which such high dilutions of particular substances can have. Hitherto, in homoeopathy, this has been merely a matter of belief; now it has been raised to the level of exact science.[20] The graphs which have been drawn leave no doubt today that the effects of the smallest particles follow a rhythmical course. I will not go into details; the work has been published and these findings can now be verified. Here I wish only to point out that even in the earthly realm the effects of enormous dilutions must be taken into account.

Here we are concerned with something which we can describe as water when we use it on a small scale. We can draw water from a river or a well and use it as water. Yes, it is water, but there is no water that consists solely of hydrogen and oxygen. It would be absurd for anyone to suppose that water consists of hydrogen and oxygen only. In the case of mineral waters and suchlike it is of course obvious that something else is present. But no water anywhere is composed solely of hydrogen and oxygen; that is only a first approximation. All water, wherever it appears, is permeated with something else. Essentially, the whole water mass of the earth is quicksilver (mercury) for the universe. Only the small quantities we use are water for us. For the universe this water is not water but quicksilver.

Hence we can begin by saying with respect to the hydrosphere in relation to water that we are dealing with a drop of quicksilver in the cosmos. Embedded in this drop of quicksilver there are, naturally, mineral substances — all the substances found on earth. They represent the solid mass of the earth, and they tend to assume their own special forms. Thus there is quicksilver in the structure as a whole. Ordinary metallic quicksilver, one might say, is only the symbol produced by nature for the general activity of quicksilver, producing a definite spherical form. Embedded in the whole sphere are the metallic crystals, with the manifold variety of their own distinctive forms. Hence we have before us this formation of earth, water, air; and its tendency, as I have said, is to assume a spherical form with individual crystal forms within it. Even if we single out the air which surrounds the earth as its atmosphere, we can never speak simply of air, for air always has a tendency to contain warmth in some degree; the air is permeated with warmth. Thus we must add this fourth element, warmth, which permeates the air.

Now this warmth which enters the air from above carries primarily within it the sulphur process it has received from the cosmos. And to the sulphur process is added the mercurial process as I have described in connection with the hydrosphere. Thus we have: air-warmth, the sulphur process; water-air, the mercurial process.

Mercury (quicksilver) as a drop, upheld by a balance of cosmic forces. From Mutus liber *(1702).*

If we now turn towards the inner part of the earth we come to the acid formation process and especially to the salt process, for the salts derive from the acids; and this is what the earth really wants to be. Hence when we look up into the cosmos we are really looking at the sulphur process. When we consider the tendency of the earth to form itself into a cosmic water drop we are really looking at the mercurial process. And if we turn our gaze to the solid earth underfoot, which in spring gives rise to all that we see as growing, sprouting life, we are looking at the salt process.

This salt process is all-important for the life and growth of spring. For in taking shape out of the seeds, the roots of plants depend for their whole growth on their relationship to the salt formed in the soil. It is these salt formations in the widest sense of the term, the deposits within the crust of the earth, which give substance to the roots and enable them to act as the earthly foundation of plant life.

Thus in turning back to the earth we encounter the salt process. This is what the earth makes of itself in the depths of winter, whereas in summer there is much more inter-mingling. For in summer the air is shot through with sulphurizing processes, which also occur in lightning and thunder; they penetrate far down, so that the whole course of the season is sulphurized. Then we come to Michaelmas, to the time when the sulphur process is driven back by meteoric iron. During summer, too, the salt process mingles with the atmosphere, for the growing plants carry the salts up through their leaves and blossoms right up into the new seeds. Naturally we find the salts widely distributed in the plant. They etherealize themselves in the essential oils, and so on; they approach the sulphurizing process. The salts are carried up through the plants; they stream out and become part of the essence of the atmosphere.

In high summer, then, we have a mingling of the mercurial element, always present in the earth, with the sulphurizing and salt-forming elements. If at this season we stand here on earth, our head actually projects into a mixture of sulphur, mercury and salt, while the arrival of midwinter means that each of these three principles reverts to its own inner condition. The salts are drawn back into the inner part of the earth, and the tendency for the hydrosphere to assume a spherical shape reasserts itself—imaged in winter by the snow mantle that covers parts of the earth. The sulphur process withdraws, so that there is no particular occasion to observe it. In place of it, something else comes to the fore during the depths of the winter season.

The plants have developed from spring to autumn, finally concentrating themselves in their seeds. What is this seeding process? When plants run to seed, they are doing what we are constantly doing in a dull human way when we use plants for food. We cook them. Now the development of a plant to blossom and then to seed production is nature's cookery; it encounters the sulphur process. The plants grow up and out into the sulphur process. They are most strongly sulphurized when summer is at its height. When autumn draws on, this combustion process comes to an end.

In the organic realm, of course, everything is different from the processes we observe in their coarse inorganic form, but the outcome of every combustion process is ash. And in addition to salt formation, which comes from quite another quarter and is needed within the earth, we must add everything that falls to the earth from the blossoming and seeding of plants as a result of the cooking or combustion process. This falling of ash—just as ash falls in our stoves—

plays an important role that is usually overlooked. For in the course of seed formation—which is fundamentally a combustion process—the seeding products are continually showering down on the earth, so that from October onwards the earth is quite impregnated with this form of ash.

If therefore we observe the earth in the depths of winter, we have first the internal tendency to salt formation. Besides this we have the mercurial shaping process in its most strongly marked form. And while in high summer we have to pay attention to the sulphurizing process in the cosmos outside the earth, in winter we now have the ash-forming process. As you can see, its culmination at Christmas is prepared in advance from Michaelmas onwards. The earth is gradually more and more consolidated, so that in midwinter it becomes really a cosmic body expressing itself in mercurial formation, salt formation, ash formation. What does this signify for the cosmos?

Now, if we can suppose that a flea, let us say, were to become an anatomist and were to study a bone, it would have in front of it minute pieces of bone, because the flea itself is so small and it would be examining the bone from a flea's perspective. The flea would then discover that in the bone there is calcium phosphate in an amorphous condition, with carbon dioxide, lime and so forth. But our flea anatomist would never come to the point of realizing that the fragment of bone is only a small part of a complete skeleton. Certainly the flea jumps, but in studying the tiny piece of bone he would never get beyond it. Similarly, it would not help a human geologist or mineralogist to be able to jump about like a gigantic earth flea. In studying the mountain ranges of the earth, which in their totality represent a skeleton, he would still be working on a minute scale. The flea would never arrive at describing the skeleton as a whole; he would hack out a tiny piece with his tiny hammer. Suppose this were a tiny piece of collarbone. Nothing in the constituents of the little piece, calcium carbonate, calcium phosphate, and so on, would reveal to the flea that it belonged to a collarbone, still less that it was part of a complete skeleton. The flea would have hacked off a tiny piece and would then describe it from his own flea perspective, just as a human being describes the earth when somewhere — let us say in the Dornach hills — he has hacked out a piece of Jura limestone. Then he describes this piece and works up his findings into mineralogy, geology, and so on. It is still the same flea standpoint, though on a larger scale.

This is not the way to arrive at the truth. We need to recognize that the earth is a single whole, most firmly consolidated during winter through its salt formation, its mercurial formation and its ash formation. We must then ask what the whole nature of the earth signifies when we look at it not from the flea's point of view, but in relation to the cosmos.

Let us first consider salt formation, taking this in the widest sense to mean a physical deposit, exemplified in the way ordinary cooking salt, dissolved in a glass of water, will separate out as a deposit on the bottom of the glass. (I will not go into the chemical side of this, though the result would be the same if I did.) Now a salt deposit of this kind has the characteristic of being porous to the spirit. Where there is a salt deposit, the spiritual element has a clear field of entry. In midwinter, accordingly, when the earth consolidates itself through salt formation, the effect is first of all that the elemental beings who are united with the earth have what one might call an agreeable abode within. But spiritual elements of another kind are also drawn in from the cosmos and are able to dwell in the salt crust which lies immediately below the earth's surface. Here, in this salt crust, the moon forces are particularly active—I mean the remains of those moon forces which were left behind, as I have often mentioned, when the moon separated from the earth.

These moon forces are active in the earth chiefly because of the salt present in it. So in winter—beneath the snow cover which pulls in one direction towards the quicksilver form, and in the other direction passes down into the salt element—we have the solid earth substance, the salt, permeated with spirituality. In winter, the earth does indeed become spiritual in itself, particularly through the consolidating influence of its salt content.

Now water—that is, cosmic quicksilver—has the internal tendency to shape itself spherically. We can see this internal tendency everywhere. And because of this the earth in midwinter is enabled not only to solidify through its salt content and to permeate the salt with spirit, but also to vivify the spiritualized substance and to lead it over into the realm of life. In winter the whole surface of the earth is reinvigorated. The quicksilver principle, working into the spiritualized salt, activates everywhere this tendency towards new life. Below the earth's surface in winter, there is a tremendous re-enlivening of the earth's capacity to produce life.

This life, however, would become moon life, for it is chiefly the moon forces that are active in it. But because ash falls down from the seeds of plants, so that everything I have just described is impregnated with ash, something is present which keeps the whole process under the control of the earth. The plants have striven upwards into the sulphur process and out of this process the ash has descended. This is what draws the plant back to earth after it has striven up into the etheric and spiritual realm. So in the depths of winter we have on the earth's surface not only the tendency to absorb the spirit and to reinvigorate itself, but also the tendency to transform what is of a moon character into earth character. Through the remains of the fallen ash, the moon is compelled to promote earthly life not moon life.

Now let us turn from the earth's surface and look at the air that surrounds the earth. It is always of the utmost importance for the air, but especially in the depths of winter, that the sun radiates warmth and light through it — though the light is less relevant to our immediate considerations.

You see, science always treats things in isolation as they never are in reality. Air, we are told, consists of oxygen and nitrogen and other elements. But in fact this is not so; the air is not made up merely of oxygen and nitrogen, for it is always rayed through by the sun. That is the reality; air is always permeated in the daytime by the activity of the sun.

And what does this activity signify? It signifies that the air up above is always seeking to tear itself away from the earth. If salt formation, mercurial formation and ash formation were alone active, then nothing but earth activity would exist. But up above, earth activity is transmuted into cosmic activity because the actions striving upwards from the earth are taken up into the activity of sun and air. The power to work on its own accord in the realm of life and spirit is taken away from the earth. The sun makes its power felt in everything that grows and sprouts upwards from the earth. And so, in a certain region above the earth, a quite special tendency is apparent to spiritual vision. On the earth itself everything seeks to become spherical; in this upper region the sphere is continually impelled to flatten out into a plane. Naturally it will tend to resume its spherical shape, but up there the spherical is always inclined to flatten out. The upper influences would really like to break up the earth, to disintegrate it, so that everything might become a flat surface, spread out there in the cosmos.

If this were to happen, the earth's activities would disappear completely and up above we would have a kind of air in which the stars would be active. This is very plainly expressed in man himself. What do we get as human beings from the sun-filled air above? We breathe it in and as a result the activity of the sun extends right into us, downwards in a sense, but chiefly upwards. Through our head we are continually drawn away from the influences of the earth, and for this reason our head is able to participate in the whole cosmos. Our head would really always like to go out into the region where the plane prevails. If our head belonged only to the earth, especially in wintertime, our whole experience of thinking would be different. We would then have the feeling that all our thoughts wished to take a rounded shape. In fact they do not; they have a certain lightness, adaptability, fluidity, and this we owe to the characteristic incursion of the activity of the sun.

Here we have the second tendency, in which the sun activity intervenes in earthly activity. But this is at its weakest in winter. If we were to go still further out, something else would come into the picture. Then we would no longer be dealing with the activity of the sun but only with the activity of the stars, for the stars in their turn have a great influence on our head. Inasmuch as the sun gives us back to the cosmos, the stars have their own deeply penetrating influence on our head and thus on the whole formation of the human organism.

But now I must tell you that what I have just been describing no longer holds good today, for in a certain way human beings have emancipated themselves in their development and their whole evolution from the earth's activities. If we were to go back to the ancient Lemurian time, or especially to the Polarian time that preceded it, we would find a quite different state of affairs. We would observe that everything that occurred on the earth had a great influence on the human organism. You will indeed have gathered this from the account of the evolution of the earth given in my *Occult Science*.[21] In those early times we would find humankind placed in the very midst of the activities I have described. Next I will describe how human beings have emancipated themselves from all of this.

Beyond nature consciousness: the spiritual goal

Generally speaking, people nowadays feel they can enter into the life of nature only in the season of growth, of germination, budding, flowering and fruit bearing. Even if they cannot fully experience all this, they have a more sympathetic awareness of it than of the autumn season of fading and withering. But in truth we deserve to rejoice in the season of spring growth only if we can enter also into the time when summer wanes and autumn approaches, the season of sinking down and dying that comes with winter. And if at midsummer we rise inwardly in a cosmic waking sleep with the elemental beings to the regions where planetary activity in the outer world can be inwardly experienced, then we ought also to lower ourselves down under the frost and snow mantle of winter so that we enter into the secrets of the womb of the earth during midwinter; and we ought to participate in the fading and dying off in nature which occurs when autumn begins.[22]

If, however, we are to participate in this waning of nature, just as we do in nature's growing time, we must learn to experience the dying away of nature in our own inner being. For if a person becomes more sensitive to the secret workings of nature, and thus participates actively in nature's germination and fruit bearing, it follows that he will also experience the effects of autumn in the outer world in a living way. But it would be comfortless for a human being if he could experience this only in the form it takes in nature, if he were to achieve the same type of consciousness of nature in relation to the secrets of autumn and winter which he easily does with regard to the secrets of spring and summer. When the events of autumn and winter draw on, when Michaelmas comes, he certainly must enter sensitively into the processes of fading and dying. But he must not, as he does in summer, give himself over to a consciousness of nature. On the contrary, he must then devote himself to self-consciousness. In the time when external nature is dying, he must oppose consciousness of nature with the force of self-consciousness.

And then the form of Michael will stand before us again.[23] If, under the impulse of anthroposophy, a person enters thus into the enjoyment of nature, the consciousness of nature, but then also awakes in himself an autumnal self-consciousness, the picture of Michael with the dragon will stand majestically before him, revealing in picture form the overcoming of the consciousness of nature by self-consciousness when autumn draws near. This will come about if humanity can experience not only an inner spring and summer but also a dying, death-bringing inner autumn and winter. Then it will be possible for the picture of Michael with the dragon to appear again as a powerful imagination, summoning humanity to inner activity.

This picture expresses something very powerful for a person who through present-day spiritual knowledge wrestles his way through to an experience of it. For when after St John's-tide July, August and September draw on, he will come to realize how he has been living through a waking sleep of inner planetary experience together with the earth's elemental beings, and he will become aware of what this really signifies. It signifies an inner process of combustion, but we must not picture it as being like external combustion. All the processes that take a definite form in the outer world take place also within the human organism, but in a different way. And so it is a fact that the changing course of the year is reflected in these inner processes.

The inner process that occurs during high summer is the permeation of the organism by what crudely may be described in the material world as sulphur. When a person lives with the summer sun and its effects, he experiences a sulphurizing process in his physical and etheric being. The sulphur that he bears within him as a useful substance has a special importance for him in high summer, quite different from its importance at other seasons. It becomes a kind of combustion process. It is natural for mankind that the sulphur process in us at midsummer should be specially enhanced. Material substances in different beings have secrets not dreamt of by materialistic science. Everything physical and etheric in us thus glows at midsummer with inward sulphur fire, to use Jakob Boehme's expression. It is a gentle, intimate process, imperceptible to ordinary consciousness, but—as is generally true of other such processes—it has a tremendous and decisive significance for events in the cosmos.

Although this sulphurizing process in human bodies at midsummer is so mild and gentle and imperceptible to humankind itself, it has very great importance for the evolution of the cosmos. A great deal happens out there in the cosmos when in summer human beings shine inwardly with the sulphur process. It is not only the physically visible glow-worms[24] which shine out around St John's Day. For other planets the inner being of mankind then begins to shine, becoming visible as a being of light to the etheric eyes of other planetary beings. That is the sulphurizing process. At the height of summer, human beings begin to ray out into cosmic space as brightly for other planetary beings as glow-worms shine with their light in the meadows at St John's time.

From the perspective of the cosmos, this is a majestically beautiful sight, for it is in glorious astral light that human beings shine out into the cosmos during high summer. But at the same time it gives occasion for the ahrimanic power to draw near to mankind. For this power is very closely related to the sulphurizing process in the human organism. We can see how, on the one hand, human beings shine out into the cosmos in the St John's light, and on the other how the dragon-like serpent form of Ahriman winds its way among human beings shining with astral light, and tries to ensnare and embrace them, to draw them down into the realm of subconscious sleep and dreams. Then, caught in this web of illusion, they would become world dreamers, and in this condition they would be a prey to the ahrimanic powers. All this has significance for the cosmos also.

And when in high summer meteors fall in great showers of cosmic iron from a particular constellation, then this cosmic iron, which carries an especially powerful healing force, is the weapon which the gods bring to bear against Ahriman[25] as, dragon-like, he tries to coil round the shining forms of human beings. The force which falls on the earth in meteoric iron is indeed a cosmic force whereby the higher gods endeavour to gain a victory over the ahrimanic powers when autumn comes on. And this majestic display in cosmic space, when the August meteor showers stream down into human beings shining in astral light, has its counterpart — so gentle and apparently so small — in a change that occurs in the human blood. The human blood, which is in truth not so material as present-day science imagines but is permeated throughout by impulses of soul and spirit, is rayed through by the force that is carried as iron into the blood and combats anxiety, fear and hate there. The processes set going in every blood corpuscle when the force of iron shoots into it are the same, on a minute human scale, as those which take place when meteors fall in a shining stream through the air. This penetration of human blood by the anxiety-dispelling force of iron drives fear and anxiety out of the blood.

And just as the gods with their meteors wage war on the spirit who would like to spread fear over all the earth with his coiling serpent form, and just as they cause iron to irradiate this fear-tainted atmosphere which is at its peak when autumn approaches or when summer wanes, so the same process occurs inwardly in human beings when their blood is permeated with iron. We can comprehend these

The archangel Michaël mastering the dragon. Occult seal by Rudolf Steiner and Clara Rettich

things only if we understand their inner spiritual significance on the one hand, and recognize how the sulphur process and the iron process in mankind are connected with corresponding events in the cosmos on the other.

A person who looks out into space and sees a shooting star should say to himself, with reverence for the gods: 'What is happening in the great expanse of space has its minute counterpart continuously in myself. Out there are the shooting stars, while in every one of my blood corpuscles iron is taking form; my life is full of shooting stars, miniature shooting stars.' And this inner fall of shooting stars, which in truth signifies the life of the blood, is especially important when autumn approaches, when the sulphur process is at its peak. For when human beings are shining like glow-worms in the way I have described, then the counter-force is present also, for millions of tiny meteors are sparkling inwardly in their blood.

This is the connection between the inner human being and the universe. And then we can see how, especially when autumn is approaching, there is a great raying upwards of sulphur from the nervous system towards the brain. One could say that the whole human being can then be seen as a sulphur-illuminated phantom.

But raying into this bluish-yellow sulphur atmosphere come the meteor swarms from the blood. That is the other phantom. While the sulphur phantom rises in clouds from the lower part of the human being towards the head, the iron-forming process rays out from his head and pours like a stream of meteors into the life of the blood.

Such is the human being when Michaelmas draws near. And we must learn to make conscious use of the meteoric force in our blood. We must learn to keep the Michael festival by making it a festival of fearlessness, a festival of inner strength and initiative, a festival for the commemoration of selfless self-consciousness.

Just as at Christmas we celebrate the birth of the Redeemer and at Easter the death and resurrection of the Redeemer, and as at St John's-tide we celebrate the outpouring of human souls into cosmic space, so at Michaelmas — if the Michael festival is to be rightly understood — we must celebrate what lives spiritually in the sulphurizing and meteorizing process within us and appears to human consciousness in its whole soul and spiritual significance especially at Michaelmas. Then a person can tell himself: 'You will be master of this process, which otherwise takes its natural course outside your consciousness, if — just as you bow down thankfully before the birth of the Redeemer at Christmas and experience Easter with a deep inner response — you learn to experience how at this autumn festival of Michael there should grow in you everything that opposes love of ease, opposes anxiety, and encourages the unfolding of inner initiative and free, strong, courageous will.' The festival of strong will — that is how we should conceive of the Michael festival. If we do that, then the Michael festival will shine out in its true colours if our knowledge of nature consists of true, spiritual and human self-consciousness.

But before humankind can think of celebrating the Michael festival, there will have to be a renewal in human souls. It is the renewal of our whole soul disposition that should be celebrated at the Michaelmas festival — not as an outward or conventional ceremony, but as a festival that renews the whole inner human being.

Then on the basis of all I have described, the majestic image of Michael and the dragon will arise once more. It will paint itself out of the cosmos. The dragon paints itself for us, forming its body out of bluish-yellow sulphur streams. We see it taking shape in shimmering clouds of radiance out of the sulphur vapours; and over the dragon rises the figure of Michael with his sword.

But we shall picture this properly only if we see the space where Michael displays his power and his lordship over the dragon as filled not with indifferent clouds but with showers of meteoric iron. These showers take form from the power that streams out from Michael's heart; they fuse into the sword of Michael who overcomes the dragon with his sword of meteoric iron.

If we understand what is happening in the universe and in mankind, then the cosmos itself will paint from out of its own forces. Then the artist does not lay on this or that colour arbitrarily. In harmony with divine powers and with the world that expresses their essence, he paints the whole being of Michael and the dragon as it appears before us. A renewal of the old pictures comes about if one can paint out of direct contemplation of the cosmos. Then the pictures will show what is really there, and not what fanciful individuals may somehow imagine to be a picture of Michael and the dragon.

Then human beings will come to understand these things, to reflect on them with understanding, and they will bring mind and feeling and will to meet autumn in the course of the year. Then, at the beginning of autumn, at the Michael festival, the picture of Michael with the dragon will confront us as a stark challenge, a strong spur to action, which must work on us in the midst of the events of our times. And then we shall understand how it points symptomatically to something in which the whole destiny — indeed, perhaps the tragedy — of our age is being played out.

During the last three or four centuries, we have developed magnificent natural science and far-reaching technology based on the most widely distributed material to be found on earth. We have learnt to make out of iron nearly all the most essential and important things produced by mankind in a materialistic age. In our locomotives, our factories, everywhere we see how we have built up this whole civilization on iron, or on steel, which is only iron transformed. And all the uses to which iron is put are a symptomatic indication of how we have built our whole life and outlook out of matter, and want to go on doing so.

That is, however, a downward-leading path. We can rescue ourselves from its impending dangers only if we start to spiritualize life in this very domain, if we penetrate though our environment to the spiritual level, if we turn from the iron which is used for making engines and look up again to the meteoric iron which showers down from the cosmos to the earth and is the outer material from which the power of Michael is forged. Human beings must come to see the great significance of the following words: 'Here on earth, in this epoch of materialism, you have made use of iron in accordance with the insight gained from your observation of matter. Now, just as you must transform your vision of matter through the further development of natural science into spiritual science, so you must rise from your former idea of iron to an understanding of meteoric iron, the iron of Michael's sword. And what you do there will make you whole.' This is contained in the aphorism which speaks of iron as follows:

O Man,
You shape it to your service,
You display it according to the value of its substance
In many of your products.
Yet it will only make you whole
When it reveals to you
The exalted dominion of its spirit.

That is, the exalted dominion of Michael with the sword that will be welded together in cosmic space out of meteoric iron when our materialistic civilization becomes capable of spiritualizing the power of iron into the power of Michaelic iron, giving us self-consciousness in place of mere consciousness of nature.

You have seen that it is precisely the most important requirement of our time, the Michaelic requirement, which is implicit in this inscription, this script contained in the astral light.

Notes

1   B.J. Teeter Dobbs, *Janus Face of Genius: The Role of Alchemy in Newton's Thought* (Cambridge 1991), following on from her earlier influential *The Foundations of Newton's Alchemy: or the 'Hunting of the Green Lion'* (Cambridge 1975); and now the scarcely less sensational Lawrence M. Principe, *The Aspiring Adept: Robert Boyle and his Alchemical Quest* (Princeton 1998).

2   See C. Nicholl, *The Chemical Theatre* (London 1980).

3   C.G. Jung, *Psychology and Alchemy* (London 1953).

4   Jung, op. cit. pp. 11ff.

5   See pp. 71–7.

6   J. Barrow and F.J. Tipler, *The Anthropic Cosmological Principle* (Oxford 1988).

7   Rudolf Steiner in many places characterizes the gradual evolution of human consciousness from a primitive clairvoyance, open to spiritual and creative forces in the world around, to modern self-awareness. There is loss, especially of the immediate sense of divine presence, but also gain, notably in clarity of consciousness and individual freedom out of which the spiritual must be rediscovered.

8   The Mystery rites practised in Samothrace and in ancient Ireland (Hibernia) both continued into the Christian era long after most of the ancient Mystery sites had ceased to be operative. See further Steiner, *Mystery Knowledge and Mystery Centres* (London 1997).

9   'Intelligence': nothing to do with our modern usage, but the term for the moving spirit in one of the planetary spheres that

bear the visible heavens in their orbits. John Donne famously compares the ideal of religion swaying the soul to this medieval cosmological idea:

Let man's Soule be a Spheare, and then, in this,

The Intelligence that moves, devotion is...

Donne, *Goodfriday*, 1613.

10 See further Steiner, *Christian Rosenkreutz* (Sussex 2001). For a general picture of Rosicrucianism in the evolution of the mysteries, see Steiner, *Mystery Knowledge and Mystery Centres* (Note 2, above); also Steiner, *Esoteric Christianity and the Mission of Christian Rosenkreutz* (London 2000).

11 Goethe, *Faust*, Part I, lines 358–9.

12 It may be a help to understanding what Rudolf Steiner means here if we bear in mind his own assertion that 'if we observe Saturn with physical vision we can locate it out there in cosmic space as a sort of luminous globe (leaving aside the rings). To the occultist who follows the spiritual events in the cosmos, the globe which is observed out there is not what the occultist calls Saturn. To him, Saturn is all which fills the entire space bounded by the ellipse (as it appears) of Saturn's orbit.' The same applies to the moon and the other planets: Steiner, *Spiritual Beings in the Heavenly Bodies and in the Kingdoms of Nature* (Vancouver 1981) pp. 95–6.

13 Cf. Rudolf Steiner, 'Blood is a Very Special Fluid' in *Supersensible Knowledge* (New York 1987).

14 Recently published as *How to Know Higher Worlds* (New York 1994).

15 Further aspects of this crucial experience on the path of the transformation of consciousness in Steiner, *Occult Science* (New York 1992), pp. 191ff.; also Steiner, *Mysteries of the East and of Christianity* (London 1972), pp. 15 ff.

16 Ahriman is the name used by Rudolf Steiner for the being behind the hardening, retarding, materializing power in cosmic evolution, also directly affecting human development. Without the ahrimanic power there would be no separation, individual existence or freedom. Nevertheless the human spirit must strive to use the ahrimanic power as a stimulus to development, growth and individualization without succumbing to its hardening effects. In this it may be helped, without impairing its freedom, by the powers especially of Christ and Michael (represented in the Bible as fighting the 'dragon').

17 See further *Spiritual Beings in the Heavenly Bodies*, pp. 68ff.

18 For Rudolf Steiner's concept of karma and reincarnation, see chapter 2 of his *Theosophy* (New York 1994); also *Reincarnation and Karma: Their Significance for Modern Culture* (New York 1992).

19 Here Rudolf Steiner drew on a blackboard. The drawing is reproduced as Plate I in Steiner, *The Four Seasons and the Archangels* (London 1968).

20 See E. & L. Kolisko, *Agriculture of Tomorrow* (Bornemouth 1978) and T. Schwenk, *The Basis of Potentization Research* (New York 1988).

21 For these earlier stages in the configuration of the earth and its continents, see Steiner, *Occult Science* (London 1969), pp. 191ff. (Also available as *An Outline of Esoteric Science*, New York 1997.)

22 Further guidance on how we can work actively together with the spiritual cycle of the year, see Steiner, *The Cycle of the Year as a Breathing Process of the Earth* (New York 1984).

23 The imagination of Michael, a spiritual power mastering the dragon-forces of materialism, is for Rudolf Steiner the definitive one for modern times (the 'Michael Age'). The stimulation to individual freedom and growth which the ahrimanic powers

give is also the danger besetting our era, in which we can however also freely receive the help offered to us by Michael and Christ in our spiritual struggle. See Steiner, *The Mission of the Archangel Michael* (New York 1961).

24   These creatures are known in German as *Johanni Käferchen*.

25   The ahrimanic powers (or Ahriman) are the materializing, densifying powers. They have their legitimate role in nature, and humanity too must enter their sphere so as to take part in active external life. If they are allowed to get out of balance, however, their tendency is to enslave humanity to externals, to materialism, and to produce blindness to the spirit. Michael is the good spiritual power who helps humanity, not to destroy Ahriman but to hold the balance so that Ahriman cannot imperil our freedom of moral action in the earthly sphere.

Sources

This book comprises thematic extracts from lectures by Rudolf Steiner.

'The loss of the divine and the alchemical quest' reproduces Steiner, *Mystery Knowledge and Mystery Centres* (London 1997), pp. 213–24 (translated from GA 232 in the edition of Steiner's original work).

'Mysteries of the metals' reproduces Steiner, *Mystery Knowledge and Mystery Centres*, pp. 226–38.

'The Standpoint of Human Wisdom' reproduces Steiner, *True and False Paths in Spiritual Investigation* (London 1969), pp. 75–82 (translated from GA 243 in the edition of Steiner's original work).

'Alchemy and consciousness' reproduces *True and False Paths*, pp. 58–72, 73–4.

'The Alchemy of Nature' reproduces Steiner, *The Four Seasons and the Archangels* (London 1996), pp. 15–24 (translated from GA 223 and 229 in the original edition of Steiner's work).

'Beyond nature consciousness' reproduces *The Four Seasons and the Archangels*, pp. 5–13.

Translations by Charles Davey, D.S. Osmond, A.H. Parker and Pauline Wehrle.

Suggested Further Reading

By Rudolf Steiner:

The Cycle of the Year as a Breathing Process of the Earth (New York 1984)
Eleven European Mystics (New York 1971)
Esoteric Christianity and the Mystery of Christian Rosenkreutz (London 2000)
The Four Seasons and the Archangels (London 1968)
How to Know Higher Worlds (New York 1994)
The Mission of the Archangel Michael (New York 1961)
Mystery Knowledge and Mystery Centres (London 1997)
Nature Spirits (London 1995)
Occult Science (London 1969). Also available as *An Outline of Esoteric Science* (New York 1997)
Origins of Natural Science (London and New York 1985)
Spiritual Beings in the Heavenly Bodies and in the Kingdoms of Nature (Vancouver 1981)
True and False Paths in Spiritual Investigation (London 1969)

Note Regarding Rudolf Steiner's Lectures

The lectures and addresses contained in this volume have been translated from the German, which is based on stenographic and other recorded texts that were in most cases never seen or revised by the lecturer. Hence, due to human errors in hearing and transcription, they may contain mistakes and faulty passages. Every effort has been made to ensure that this is not the case. Some of the lectures were given to audiences more familiar with anthroposophy; these are the so-called 'private' or 'members' lectures. Other lectures, like the written works, were intended for the general public. The difference between these, as Rudolf Steiner indicates in his *Autobiography*, is twofold. On the one hand, the members' lectures take for granted a background in and commitment to anthroposophy; in the public lectures this was not the case. At the same time, the members' lectures address the concerns and dilemmas of the members, while the public work speaks directly out of Steiner's own understanding of universal needs. Nevertheless, as Rudolf Steiner stresses: 'Nothing was ever said that was not solely the result of my direct experience of the growing content of anthroposophy. There was never any question of concessions to the prejudices and preferences of the members. Whoever reads these privately printed lectures can take them to represent anthroposophy in the fullest sense. Thus it was possible without hesitation — when the complaints in this direction became too persistent — to depart from the custom of circulating this material "For members only". But it must be borne in mind that faulty passages do occur in these reports not revised by myself.' Earlier in the same chapter, he states: 'Had I been able to correct them [the private lectures], the restriction *for members only* would have been unnecessary from the beginning.'

ALSO AVAILABLE IN THE 'POCKET LIBRARY OF SPIRITUAL WISDOM' SERIES

Rudolf Steiner
Atlantis
The Fate of a Lost Land and its Secret Knowledge

The Continent of Atlantis; The Moving Continents; The History of Atlantis; The Earliest Civilizations; The Beginnings of Thought; Etheric Technology — Atlantean 'Magic' Powers; Twilight of the Magicians; The Divine Messengers; Atlantean Secret Knowledge — it's Betrayal and Subsequent Fate; The Origins of the Mysteries; Atlantis and Spiritual Evolution

RSP; 112pp; 17 × 12 cm; 1 85584 079 0; pb; £7.95

Rudolf Steiner
The Holy Grail
The Quest for the Renewal of the Mysteries

From the Mysteries to Christianity; Death and Resurrection in Ancient Egypt — the Miracle of Initiation; The Mystery of Golgotha; The Mystery of the Higher Ego — the Holy Grail; The Grail and the Spiritual Evolution of Humanity; The Gnostic Crisis and the Loss of the Mysteries; Stages of Evolution — Archaic Clairvoyance; The Role of the Mysteries; The Secret of Evolution — the Holy Grail.

RSP; 96pp; 17 × 12 cm; 1 85584 074 X; pb; £7.95

Rudolf Steiner
Christian Rosenkreutz
The Mystery, Teaching and Mission of a Master

The Mystery of Christian Rosenkreutz; The Working of
Christian Rosenkreutz Today and in the Past; Christian
Rosenkreutz as the Guardian of Modern Knowledge; From
Ancient to Modern in Rosicrucian Teachings; Christian
Rosenkreutz at the 'Chymical Wedding'; The Cosmic
Mission of Christian Rosenkreutz; The Question of
'Rosicrucian' Literature.

RSP; 96pp; 17 × 12 cm; 1 85584 084 7; pb; £7.95

Rudolf Steiner
The Druids
Esoteric Wisdom of the Ancient Celtic Priests

The Sun Initiation of the Druid Priests and their Moon
Science; The Mysteries of Ancient Ireland; Celtic
Christianity—the Heritage of the Druids; Teachings of the
Mysteries—the Spirit in Nature; The Great Mysteries—the
Mystery of Christ; The Function of the Standing Stones;
Spiritual Imaginations.

RSP; 96pp; 17 × 12 cm; 1 85584 099 5; pb; £7.95

Rudolf Steiner
The Goddess
From Natura to the Divine Sophia

Rediscovering the Goddess Natura; Retracing our Steps—
Mediaeval Thought and the School of Chartres; The Goddess
Natura in the Ancient Mysteries; The Goddess in the
Beginning—the Birth of the Word; Esoteric Christianity—the
Virgin Sophia; the Search for the New Isis; The Renewal of
the Mysteries; The Modern Isis, the Divine Sophia.

RSP; 112pp; 17 × 12 cm; 1 85584 094 4; pb; £7.95